I Have Never Tasted Any Bad Ice Cream and other RANDOM OBSERVATIONS

HENRY L. BOWDEN

Published by
Looking Glass Books
730 Sycamore Street
Decatur, Georgia   30030
(404) 371-1236

Manufactured in the United States of America.
ISBN 0-9640852-4-0

RANDOM
OBSERVATIONS

Contents

Henry Bowden, always a leader, and always young

BY MAX HALL

enry Lumpkin Bowden, an unusual lawyer who was powerfully involved in the governing of both Emory University and the City of Atlanta, died on February 17, 1997. He was 86 and had become weak from many ailments, and in his last five years he had suffered from a case of shingles that doctors could not cure. But, astonishingly, in that very time of pain he was pursuing what almost amounted to a new career.

Though his beloved profession was the law, he had also been a secret lover of journalism since his college years at Emory (class of '32). And now, in the 1990s, about twice a month, he typed or dictated his own journalistic "column." He called it Random Observations.

These pieces were personal, autobiographical, and uninhibited. Each column was a string of items, short and long. In a conversational style that might be called Non-legalese Bowdenesque, he told about growing up in Atlanta; poked fun at himself as a member of the "cane gang" of old age;

described his daily habits in rather graphic detail; declared his likes and dislikes ("I have never tasted any bad ice cream"); contrasted the behavior of women and men; gave candid opinions and advice on this and that; and delivered jokes and jingles he made up, picked up, or pulled out of a long memory. Many of his items had the form and quality of literary essays.

For more than six years Henry sent Random Observations to some of his friends. He wrote them for amusement, not for publication. True, the Meriwether Vindicator, in Meriwether County, Georgia, printed excerpts under his name. (He had not sought this, but didn't protest.) Many of those on his mailing list had heard him make after-dinner speeches and would argue that he was the world's best storyteller. Random Observations gave them the feeling they could "hear Henry talking."

One of his friends, James T. Laney, former president of Emory, completed a four-year term as U.S. Ambassador to the Republic of Korea at about the time Henry died. Laney returned from Asia just in time to speak at the funeral. Of Henry he said, "He has rightly been called Mr. Emory, and with his passing, that title will have to be retired."

Laney also spoke about Henry's extraordinary personality, how he "remained perennially young," how he "brought so much pleasure and joy to life." Then Laney told of the times when Random Observations arrived periodically at the Ambassador's Residence in Seoul. He said that he and his wife, Berta, loved to open the bulky envelope and read its contents aloud. "It was as though we had a visit with Henry. And we would chuckle and smile and think how much we missed that — that *touch*."

The book you have in your hands contains an abundant selection of Random Observations, in which the items have been rearranged into chapters, by topic. The aim of the publisher, Dick Parker of Looking Glass Books, is to give wider circulation to the Bowden touch.

Henry Bowden was born in Atlanta on July 23, 1910, and grew up on Moreland Avenue. As a boy he already exhibited the breezy good humor that was to endear him to people later in life. While attending Boys' High and Emory he held many jobs. For example, he worked in a peach-packing shed, in the Atlanta Crackers' ballpark presiding over the manually operated scoreboard, and in the sports department of an Atlanta paper. (Don't miss the item on page 15 where he tells about his jobs.)

It was at Emory that he developed leadership. He was probably the best-known and most honored student in the University. His many activities included intramural basketball and baseball and the editorship of The Emory Wheel. For several years he wrote an exuberant column for the Wheel called "Here's the Dope." Looking back now, one can see that "Here's the Dope" was a direct ancestor of Random Observations.

Typically, in "Here's the Dope" he invented nicknames for people. A pitcher on his class baseball team, for example, became "Blind Man" Tucker. This nicknaming continued in his later life. He addressed his friend Bishop William R. Cannon as "Big Willie." His friend Griffin Bell was "Ding-Dong," and when Bell was Attorney General of the United States the security officers at the Justice Department, opening letters from Bowden beginning "Dear Ding-Dong," thought they were from "some crackpot." Henry's cook was "Phi Beta." His secretary was "Mrs. Black" (her real name was Debbie Schwartz). His grandson Henry III was "Three-Eye." Boisfeuillet Jones was "Bull's Foot." Harvey Hill was "The Goop." For complicated reasons, President Laney was sometimes "Joe Frank" and sometimes "Aloysius." So far as I know, his friends accepted their new names complacently. Bowden's own lifelong nickname, of uncertain origin, was "Hinky."

Hinky Bowden was in the class of '34 at the Emory Law School, though he finished his courses in 1933 and was admitted to the bar in August of that year. In 1937 he married Ellen Fleming. In 1939 he and Hamilton Lokey formed the law firm of Lokey & Bowden. During the war Bowden served in the Army Quartermaster Corps, assigned to Atlanta. In June 1947, when he was only 36, he became president of the Atlanta Bar Association. That same year, he was appointed to Emory's Board of Trustees. Ten years later he became its chairman.

Bowden's 22 years as chairman, from 1957 to 1979, made him a legend at Emory. Through personal persuasion he raised millions for the University. He made speeches for Emory in more than 50 cities. In troubled times he reconciled differences between the trustees and the faculty. In addition to board chairman, he was Emory's general counsel, and in that capacity he brought the lawsuit that overthrew a segregationist provision in Georgia's constitution and thereby enabled Emory and other private schools to enroll black students without losing their tax exemption. The American Association of University Professors gave him an award for that.

Also of historic importance for Emory was his crucial role — as board chairman — in choosing Emory presidents, including James Laney, and in recruiting energetic new board members. After leaving the board he wrote a book entitled *Boards of Trustees: Their Organization and Operation at Private Colleges and Universities* (Mercer University Press, 1982).

In that same era, Bowden handled legal affairs for the fast-growing City of Atlanta. After a spell as Associate City Attorney, he was the City Attorney from 1963 to 1976, serving under four mayors. His office was busy acquiring property for Atlanta's airport, stadium, sewers, and the system of superhighways running through the center of the city.

In an incident that attracted attention in 1966, the City Attorney and the Rev. Martin Luther King Jr. engaged in a little biblical skirmish. The city had discharged hundreds of striking firemen. King said the city should "go the second mile," as Jesus instructed in Matthew 5:41. Bowden gives us his response in his telling of the story on page 2.

Henry Bowden was a man of strong convictions. When he believed he was right he could be adamant — and resourceful in winning his point. Yet he was a sentimental man, especially when it came to family and friends. More than once in Random Observations he told of being moved to tears. He was also a playful man. Once when he was in the Quartermaster Corps he took a train trip with two other officers who hadn't met each other before. He told each of them that the other was very hard of hearing and had to be shouted to.

During the 60 years when Hinky and I corresponded, the mail deliverers must have wondered about me, for his envelopes named me as "Hon.," and often as admiral, general, ambassador, or whatnot. He ended letters with "HEITR," which meant "Hold 'em in the road." He sometimes called himself "Your groveling scrivener." Periodically he did something that much intrigued my children. That is, he sent me batches of things he salvaged from his desk or billfold, such as business cards left by visitors, outdated identification cards, old auto registrations, snapshots, swizzle sticks from cruise liners, buckeyes for good luck, and more.

Religion played a great part in Hinky's existence. He taught Sunday School most of his life, beginning, I think, in his early twenties. Some of his close friends were Methodist bishops. Bishop William Cannon spoke emotionally at his funeral — less than three months before his own death. On January 17, 1991, Hinky wrote me, "Last year I read the Bible for the 8th time and am now listening to it on tape."

Hinky loved his red pickup truck. He loved his farm in Meriwether County, visited it when he could, built a house there (with lots of help, I guess), and waged a titanic struggle with a band of beavers that kept creating an unwanted pond. Random Observations are populated not only with people, but also cows, some of which were his childhood acquaintances. He liked country music and, about a year before his death, announced in a Random Observation, "I have about decided that if I had to do it all over again, I would not be a lawyer. I decided that what I would be is a country music songwriter and I've already written my first song." He gave us that lyric, and two Randoms later he gave us another.

One of Hinky's greatest passions was travel. He loved getting out on the highway and seeing all parts of the United States. He kept a long list of the foreign countries he had visited. His wife, Ellen, was his travel companion until her death in 1986 — a death he took terribly hard. His journalistic bent caused him to write reports of his journeys and send them to friends. His account of a Panama Canal cruise with his daughter Mary Lamar in 1990 makes 40 pages, double-spaced.

I always marveled at Hinky's talent for remembering. He could recite "Casey at the Bat" without missing a line. Word for word, he remembered those funny Burma Shave rhymes that used to line the highways. He never forgot the Boy Scout Oath. He could rattle off the roll call of the high school R.O.T.C. company of which he had been First Sergeant.

The accomplishments of Henry Bowden brought him prodigious recognition. I will end this introduction by choosing just a few more examples of the honors that came his way. Not only the Atlanta Bar Association but also the Georgia Bar Association made him its president. Jimmy Carter, as governor and then in the White House, put him at the head of selection committees to advise on judicial appointments in Georgia. A discussion group called The Ten, founded in 1898 and consisting of judges, college presidents, and other leaders, made him a member in 1964 and eventually made him its "Czar." Emory University named a building after him in 1988, just across the Quadrangle from the place where he had gleefully pounded out "Here's the Dope" 60 years before.

RANDOM
OBSERVATIONS

1

The Law

Back in 1933 when I finished law school times were hard. Jobs doing most anything were few. I felt fully capable of holding one of the positions on the U.S. Supreme Court but actually had no job at all. My longtime good friend Harvey (The Goop) Hill got me a job with a fellow whom he knew named William E. Arnaud, who represented ASCAP for southern states (Georgia, Florida, Alabama and Tennessee). The ASCAP outfit were the owners of the copyrights on most all then-published music.

Federal law required a business using music to obtain permission of the copyright owner to play that music publicly for profit and if one played it for profit in such as a dance hall, moving picture show, burlesque house, or restaurant and did not have permission of the owner of the copyright, he was subject to an automatic fine of $250 for each rendition of the song. My job was to travel those four states and visiting all these different places, list the songs heard and write them a letter demanding they take out a license to use ASCAP music and if they refused to do so I would sue them.

It was interesting after winning such a case to hear an elderly, usually bald-headed and fully robed U.S. federal judge intone from the bench such as this in deep, judicial tones: "Mr. Hackenbush, it having been proven adequately to the court that you did on July 23, 1935, at your club of business named 'The Big Blonde, Cha, Cha Night Club,' play for profit a certain song as to which you did not own the copyright or have permission from the copyright owner so to use, you are hereby fined the full sum of two hundred and fifty dollars with all costs of the court assessed against you, the name of the said song being 'How Am I Doing, Hey, Hey, Twee, Twee, Twee, Twa, Twa.' "

My compensation (salary) in this first job was $75 per month which was seventy-five dollars greater than I earned the preceding month. After several months my stipend was increased to an unbelievable $100 per month.

THE HEART OF THE MATTER

When I first began law practice a man came in one day and said, "Lawyer Bowden, I have been charged with stealing some bicycles. I need a good lawyer to handle my case." I had no clients and was glad he came in, but I said to him this: "Goliath, I will be glad to represent you, but you first tell me whether or not you did steal those bicycles."

Goliath's reply was, "Lawyer Bowden, first thing right off the bat you done touched on the weakest part of my case."

A SET-TO WITH MARTIN LUTHER KING JR.

Back in the sixties when my friend Ivan Allen was mayor, I had the very doubtful distinction of being city attorney. The firemen went on strike. There was a big hassle. The firemen asked Martin Luther King Jr., then in his prime, to intercede for them as spokesman and he asked the mayor to meet with him at the fire department headquarters. Ivan talked to me and said he was not going but wanted me to go. I went. I said,

"Dr. King, what is it you want?" and his reply was from the Bible. He said he wanted the city to "go the extra mile" with these firemen and to give in to their demands which, as I recall it, had to do with raises and other issues. I told him that when they struck the city offered to take them back and to talk about their grievances. They refused to stop striking. Then the city gave them another invitation and extended the time for several days. They still refused to return to work. The city was in danger should a fire break out. Then the mayor, after talking with me, decided to prefer charges against the men to try them for failure to carry out their duties. Trial times were set and he said again to them he would forgive them if they returned to work before trial. None came back to work and none showed up for trial. So I quoted scripture to Martin Luther King Jr. and said he might recall that when Christ was asked whether or not a man should forgive another seven times his reply was, no it should be something like 70 times 7 times, as I remembered it. I told him we had gone beyond the extra mile, we had forgiven 70 times 7 times. They were fired. Those not striking were promoted to the vacancies and those who struck if they applied again were hired at the lower levels in subordinate positions.

⸻

PARTNERSHIP [SPRING 1996]

Some partnerships last a long time. Others break up soon. And I have one formula for a fine lasting association of the type that Ham Lokey and I had. We formed Lokey and Bowden on the third day of April, 1939, and it remained a wonderfully fine relationship between Ham Lokey and myself until we terminated it in 1995. I could not have selected a finer person to have as my ally in the practice of law than Ham. He was always honest, straightforward, and fair.

When we got together, we had nothing in writing. We simply shook hands and said, "Beginning tomorrow morning, April 4, 1939, everything that comes into the firm is half yours and half mine."

I said, "I will keep all the books reflecting income and the like, if any, and Ham, you will look after the library."

So I signed all my notes to him "Bookkeeper" and he signed his to me "Librarian."

Ham is absolutely true blue, never allowing himself to take any shortcuts or improper approaches to victory. Ham did a lot of work for the Board of Regents of the state university system and I did work for the City of Atlanta and Emory University. What wonderful years and what wonderful experiences we had. What a great fellow Ham Lokey has been.

Pollard Turman was to have been another partner with us but he unfortunately was offered a job which we advised him to take because it assured him of a regular income and we had no such assurances. He would have been equally a partner with Ham and me.

Ham is still living although I'm sorry to say he has suffered with Alzheimer's to some degree in the past few years. I'm still living too and have avoided Alzheimer's thus far. At the present time I am bedridden with shingles and have nurses 24 hours a day. But I'm still alive and I thank the Lord every day for the good friends and acquaintances I've had over the years. I may not be here too much longer since I'm 85 years old, but those years have been wonderful years to me and I thank God every day for giving me the opportunity to have enjoyed life as I have.

MORE ON PARTNERSHIP

Last month in August 1996, my longtime friend and law partner, Hamilton Lokey, died. He and I had the ideal partnership for well over 50 years. We had nothing in writing. We simply shook hands on one day, the 3rd of April. We skipped April 1 because we did not want to start the firm on April Fools' Day, and April 2 was a Sunday.

He was a great lawyer and was good at everything he undertook. He took some positions which were not always popular, but which he and others felt were proper, as did I.

He left a fine family and a host of friends and admirers, as shown by those who attended his funeral services.

Ours was a 50-50 partnership. I was in the military reserve and was called to military duty the year before Pearl Harbor. My salary was about $172 per month as a shave-tail second lieutenant. Ham kept the firm going and took the first $172 fees for himself and sent me one-half of everything else. Later, after the war was over, Ham was called back in for naval duty for some while and his salary was $400 per month. I had the privilege of reciprocating, so I took the first $400 in legal fees and sent him half of the rest. He was grateful as was I and said he could not have made it without that added compensation. I miss Ham.

FLAG BURNING

In recent days, there has been much ado about the question of whether or not there should be an amendment to the Constitution prohibiting the burning of the United States flag. Professional patriots all seem to favor it. More relaxed but still genuine patriots oppose it. I oppose it. I detest the idea of burning the flag out of protest or any animus against our government. I would not burn it in such circumstances and I would look with disdain on any person guilty of such. However, if you are to make burning the flag unconstitutional, should you not also make cutting it into shreds against the law? How about tearing it up or using an old one for a dust cloth or even dipping it in paint or dissolving it in acid? You might say the term to be used is "desecrating" the flag. Then you will have to define carefully the term "desecrating."

Burning the flag in protest against the government is simply demonstrably "saying" something. To say the same thing with words is not against the law and should not be. Why should it be if "said" by burning the flag? Freedom of expression is basic in a democracy. We must preserve that right and not try to temper it with modifications that open the way to further curtailment. Burners of the flag will, by almost 100 percent of the citizenry, be criticized and ostracized, but it would be poor policy to convict them of a crime and imprison them.

LUMPS IN THE THROAT

My father was a lawyer. He has now been dead since 1955. He and I were very close and I had a great respect, love and admiration for him. He, I am sure, had far more legal ability than I. He was 83 when he died. He served as law clerk for two Supreme Court of Georgia justices, Judge Joseph Henry Lumpkin and Judge William Fish. In fact he named me for Justice Lumpkin (Henry Lumpkin Bowden) and I always kidded that he was looking for a raise. After I entered the practice he was gradually doing less and less. As I was in the process of trying a case once I happened to look in the back of the courtroom and there sat my daddy as a spectator. The case was not one that will go down in history as one of the landmark cases in legal jurisprudence, but he just wanted to come and see "his boy" try a case. Even now as I think on it I get a lump in my throat. I loved him devotedly. I now have a fine son, Henry Lumpkin Bowden Jr. and he, too, is a lawyer. I have on occasion observed him at work with great pride and satisfaction. I still get a lump in my throat and I have decided that lumps in the throat are really wonderful things. I hope that I continue to experience them and that they do not go out of style in the next generation and those that follow. My son now has a young lad just five years old. Maybe someday my son may have the chance to have a big lump in his throat. Grandpa certainly hopes so.

BACK TO THE BEGINNING

I was in court this morning at the Fulton County Courthouse. It made me think back to the first time I was in the building "officially" and it was August 8, 1933, when I was admitted to the bar and sworn in (after finishing at Emory

Law School) by Judge Virlyn B. Moore whose son, Virlyn Jr., was with me at Emory. Strangely, years later when my son, Henry Jr., was sworn in as a lawyer, he too having been graduated from Emory Law School, Judge Moore was yet on the bench and I was present when Judge Moore also swore in Henry Jr. It may have happened in some other family but I do not know about it.

⊷

CAREERS

Do you reckon a man who ended up being an embalmer in a funeral home started out with that career in mind? I seriously doubt it. It is interesting to me how folks end up in the jobs they hold. How many started out with that in mind? I really did not know what I planned to do when I got to college. I finally decided I would probably go in either newspaper work or into general insurance (not life insurance). Emory made it possible in those dark-age years to take your last year in the college as your first year in professional school (law or medicine) and I elected to take my last college year in law because I figured one year of law might help me in any business. After that year in law I decided I liked it and so I went on and completed my law degree too and went three summers to save a whole year.

I am glad I made this decision because my chosen profession has been kind to me. I have enjoyed it all the way and have felt that it gives a person the opportunity to help someone else regularly. You don't get rich in law practice. But there are enriching experiences that are rewarding in so many other ways than financial gain.

I was never attracted toward being a CPA, stock broker, blacksmith, or shoe repairman. I could see myself as a physician but only if I did not have to cut on anyone. I felt I could go as far as applying Band-Aids and, in extreme emergencies, administering flu shots, but no cutting. I expect that most folks just sort of drift into their jobs without any predetermined desire to do what they do. Veterinarians, black-

7

smiths, jockeys, truck drivers and so many other folks have probably just drifted into the jobs they hold. After all I guess that may be the best way to go about it.

THE BEST IS YET TO BE

Along about May 1, 1995, my son Henry Jr. and I will leave where each of us is and will join together and form the new law firm of which he and I will be the only partners, to be dubbed The Bowden Law Firm. He is leaving King & Spalding, a wonderful firm, where he has now been for some 20 years and very happy, and I will leave Lokey and Bowden, where my great partner Ham Lokey and I have practiced together since 1939 (some 56 years). I was, of course, flattered when my son suggested the change to me and I will admit that I cried a bit which I am given over to much more freely now than in my balmier days. There are some things that just naturally bring on joyful, thankful, and spontaneous tears. This is one of them.

ONE YEAR

Last week marked the first year of the formation of The Bowden Law Firm of which my son, Henry, is the Senior Partner. He's got some six or eight employees and specializes in nothing but wills, personal law, family law, and the like. Fortunately for him and those working with him, of which I was supposed to be one but have been unable to fulfill that bargain, the year has been very, very encouraging and satisfactory. He loves all his employees and I hope for him they hold a deep respect.

He has certainly been a fine son to an ailing old father and I cannot express it enough by simply saying so and I have told him so many times. His wife, Jeanne, who is terrific, works with the firm since she is also an Emory Law graduate. I hope the firm continues successfully and I regret the poor old father has not been able to be a part of it as I thought I would.

2

Family

I guess that in any person's life there are things, maybe little thing to others, but which take on the aspect of big things to the person who has experienced them. One of the things that everyone really needs at some times in his life is some degree of recognition and approval for what he may have done or refrained from doing, which comes from one whom you admire and respect. I can recall several such instances in my life. One stands out in particular.

My father, though he lived in the city of Atlanta, had a real love of cows. When he was permitted back in the earlier years in the first quarter of the 20th century he kept a cow or two on his place in Atlanta, which was just a regular house and lot located on North Moreland Avenue.

Each morning he would get up early before going to work, put on old clothes and go up to what we called "the lot" at the rear end of our yard. He would feed the cow, clean up the lot and do the morning milking. He would bring the still warm milk back to the house, where my mama would strain it, cool it a bit and put it in a regular glass milk bottle of the kind then used. By that time I was up and would put a homemade canvas sack on my back, put a few bottles in it and, on my bicycle, go around our neighborhood delivering our excess to neighbors, who welcomed it. I can even remember sometimes the milk in the bottles was still warm, as there was no pasteurization in this our home production operation.

One morning while I was yet in bed, my mother (I called her Mama and never Mom, as is now done), came to my bed and said, "Son, get up in a hurry. Your father has had an accident. He fell on the ice while up at the lot and has broken his shoulder or injured it badly. You have got to take over and do the milking until he recovers." It was not a question of, "Naw, Mama, I don't want to." My mama said do it and that was it. So, I hastened to get up and go up to the lot. It involved taking not only the milk bucket and a quart cup, but also a bucket of hot water and rags, so as to wash off and clean thoroughly the cow's bag making sure that all of the teats were clean and pink.

Then I always put some cottonseed meal and hulls in the feed box so the cow could be eating as I milked, to keep her mind off what I was doing. I had a device I also used, which my daddy had gotten from somewhere, which was an anti-kicking device. A cow's hind leg works backward from a person's. The leg moves forward as she walks and the knee bends forward. So, this device in the shape of two U-shaped pieces of metal joined by a chain, was a great thing. Put one of the U-shaped pieces over the joint just above the knee, bring the chain around in front of the legs and across and put the other U-shaped piece over the other knee joint, so that if the cow kicked, she would with one leg be pulling against the other. Don't know who got it up, but it worked and worked well. I would put this on the cow first thing.

I also tied her tail with a string to a nearby post, so she could not flick it in my face as I milked her. When, due to an occasional fly, or to my milking operations, she would become restless and not "give down" the milk as I felt she should, I would, as my dad had done, slap her gently on the flank and say, "SAAHH REDEYE" (that was her name), and she would relax and the milk

10

would flow. I also, as a measure of protection, would milk into a quart cup instead of into the big two-gallon bucket. I kept the bucket up on a shelf above my head and, when I filled the cup, I would stand up and pour it into the bigger bucket. I felt that she somehow, in spite of the anti-kicking device, might upset the bucket. So, I kept it out of her range.

My daddy was to me a great person. I was his only son. He had lost my younger brother to childhood illnesses when the lad was about six years old in 1920. I know on many occasions my father (I called him Daddy), must have felt I was never going to grow up to be able to do the things he could do. He was just about right about it, too. So, whenever my daddy seemed to approve of what I was doing, it made me feel especially good.

While he was ill with his broken shoulder, I performed his chores of milking and the like every day. It was winter time and cold and all this had to be done early in order that I could get off to school on time.

He never said to me that he was proud of the way I had taken over in his illness, but when I would come back to the house and bring in the milk, I could see him as he sat there. He had no words of communication to say, but he did not need to have. I could see on his face a calmness, a serenity that was obvious and a look of complete approval and, yes, pride, I am sure, in the realization that I was doing his job. That silent look of approval, that calmness and serenity, and that quiet uncriticizing expression meant then, and means to me now, more than anyone can ever know. I shall never forget it as long as I live.

These things should have carryover into the next generation or to friends. It is not so much what a person says which often means the most. It is in the reaction and facial expression, the look in the eyes, the relaxed attitude of appreciation and approval that speaks so much more volubly than any words might.

These all came to me from my father, now dead these thirty-five years, but those things I shall never forget.

HE'D BE PROUD

At a family gathering recently, my son said to me that so many of the folks there were descendants of my grandpa, John Malachi Bowden. He said there were no bums, criminals, deadbeats, dope addicts, chiselers, or drunks present. He and I agreed that old Malachi would have been proud in a way. True, he would not have liked the way most of us looked but he could take pride that we had not jumped the tracks.

MOTHERHOOD

A woman literally goes down into the valley of the shadow of death to bring forth a wee human being. She sees it for the first time and after counting its toes and fingers holds it for the first time to her breast and hears the little new life making soothing, satisfying, and wonderful sounds that only an infant can make. And then from the most basic of instincts the little one begins to nurse at its mother's breast and she realizes that she is now providing the life giving nurture and sustenance to this human created by and in the image of God. This it seems to me must be the most complete and satisfying feeling of fulfillment that can be experienced by a human being. Without this process the world would die as it applies to humanity. Fathers are a necessary part of the process but they are only supportive and really background for the glorious event. It is no wonder that there is nothing to equal mother love and that we humans almost to a person have a most profound and deep seated adoration for our mothers. And strangely the memory of the long months of sometimes uncomfortable pregnancy and the pangs of childbirth seem to fade away and these same mothers seem to welcome again and again the opportunity to experience the same fulfillment. What great persons mothers are.

MOTHER LOVE

Human relationships are the most important things there are, to my way of thinking. By no means the least important of these human relationships is that of parenthood. The father "begets" a child and that, of course, is a pleasant experience, but a mother "brings forth a child" — develops a human being in her body and brings it forth into the world completely helpless and completely dependent.

Somehow there goes immediately from that new mother to that new little baby, the greatest surge of love known to humankind. It is, as I observe it, a mixture of adoration, affection and tenderness which carries with it a willingness to sacrifice for the life and welfare of that infant. It extends to the point that the mother is almost immediately perfectly willing to sacrifice her own life for that of her child. It is beautiful and tender.

A father also loves the child but his love, which similarly is deep, carries with it the aspect of pride and joy that a child is born into the world. The Bible, you will recall, refers to faith, hope and charity (love), and it says that the greatest of these is love. And I add that I think the greatest of loves is that which a mother has for her child.

THE GREAT INFLUENCE OF LITTLE THINGS

Have you ever thought about the seemingly little, trivial things of really insignificant nature that cast a decisive, long time and significant influence on your life? Here is an example. One summer's day in 1931 a friend, Sanborn Cooper, who was a classmate of mine at Boys' High School and Emory, told me he had a date that night with a girl who had a visitor and that he would like for me to go with him to be a date for the visitor. I gladly told him I would. He picked me up that night in his daddy's Flint automobile. They no longer make it but it was a well known one in those days. When he came he said that I had a date with the girl and he had a date with the visitor. That reversed what I was told in the morning but I knew neither so it made no difference. That is what we did. The girl was Ellen Fleming. I was stricken. I knew she was the one and after that we courted for six years as she finished high school and college (she was 15 when we met) and while I finished law school and started practicing law. But suppose I had been the one to have the date with the visitor? What a great difference in things some small and seemingly trivial thing can make. It was 49 and a half years and four children later that she died. Thank goodness for trivial accidents.

13

MY ELLEN

She was so shy but oh so pretty when first we met in the late spring of 1931. And oh how I was stricken. I told my mama the next morning that I had met "her" the night before. Mama asked how I knew and I said that I just knew and that was all there was to it. She was five feet seven inches tall and a dark blonde with all of the grace you could imagine. There was really heaven in her smile and undiluted beauty in her face. I think our feelings for each other were mutual. She was 15 when we met and I was 20. The next month I was 21 and she gave me a birthday party at her home with several of our friends attending. I never was able to understand how she could have any interest in me but understood fully why I had interest in her. She was wonderful and remained so until her death on that Sunday morning November 16, 1986. What a girl, what a woman, what a lady and really what a princess she was.

I attended her high school graduation from Washington Seminary and she said she knew I was there because she heard me cough. I was in the balcony and must have had a distinctive cough for her to have heard it. I smoked in those days but thank goodness saw the light and gave up that awful habit. She started to college at Florida State College for Women (now Florida State) in Tallahassee on September 11, 1933, and I started the practice of law that same day. I put her on a train on Saturday night the 9th of September at the old Terminal station. I along with several other of her suitors was there. I told her that if she would go off and get her degree and come on back we would get married. She did just that. I attended her college graduation. She came on back home with that degree and 30 days later we were married at the First Presbyterian Church in Atlanta. Dr. William V. Gardner conducted the ceremony.

Of our marriage we were blessed with four wonderful children. How could a man ask for more in a wife than intelligence, beauty, grace, charm, magnificent motherhood, a devoted Christian and a loving and companionable wife and friend. Her children worshipped her and we know where she is now. It is my fervent hope and prayer that although undeserving of it I may some day rejoin her up there.

3

Growing Up

When I was coming along we had no money of any recognizable amount and the same held for others in the neighborhood. Thus, I always sought to get some job of some kind to enable me to be a bit more affluent. Got to thinking about the jobs I have had and these are some of them.

I started out milking the family cows. Then delivered the excess production beyond our needs to our neighbors.

Kids used to set up what we called drink stands by the curbing in front of their homes. The "stand" consisted simply of two boxes or orange crates (one on top of the other) and a bucket with some ice in it into which you placed the Coca-Colas or other soft drinks we sold. Cokes were standard but they had some big drinks sold at the same price which we kids termed "belly wash." Each crate of soft drinks cost eighty cents and there were 24 in each case so you sold the case for a total of $1.20 and the 40 cents was your profit. This went on all summer long up and down the street. It was fun and provided some bit of cash.

Clerked Friday afternoon and Saturday at the grocery store (A&P or L.W. Rogers) and took in $3.50 for the two days.

Carried an Atlanta Journal paper route. It was number 112 and it had about 100 papers to deliver each afternoon rain or shine. The papers were dropped off by the street car motorman at my corner and I began the job. I delivered the papers, folding them and tossing them on the porches. There was a certain way we carriers folded the papers and throwing them was really fun. I also collected from the subscribers the cost of the papers. The cost was twenty cents per week. That was ten dollars and forty cents per year if I have figured it correctly (I went to night school and never could add and subtract very well in the daytime).

Sold peanuts and other goodies at Spiller Field [later renamed Ponce de Leon Park] where the Atlanta Crackers played. The standard cry was, "PEEEENUTS, CIGARS, CIGARETTES AND CHEWING GUM." Also sold soft drinks and the call was, "CO-COLA, LEMON, ORANGE AND GRAPE HERE." We were paid ten percent of what we sold. Moved on up to keeping the scoreboard out in center field. It was not electric either. At that time a fellow named Earl Mann was selling cushions in the lobby of the park so as to provide patrons of a soft seat for the game. Earl ended up owning the Crackers and I was his lawyer. I am sure stranger things have happened but not to me.

For three separate summers I journeyed to Lee Pope, Georgia (near Fort Valley), to work in peach packing operations. I was immediately branded as a city slicker and I guess sort of a weak backed person. The test of manhood was whether or not the person could "shoulder" a keg of nails, weighing 100 pounds. The gang stood around to see me try and I was determined not to fail. I got hold of it, put it up on my shoulder and thereafter was considered "one of the gang" to my great glee.

I then became a sports contributor to the Atlanta Georgian, a Hearst paper no longer in existence. After that I went each Saturday and tabulated final football scores for that same paper under sports editor Ed Danforth, one of the greatest. I would always mark the copy for the printer as follows: "set in 6 point agate, flush right and left." That was over 60 years ago but I can even now remember those days and the names of some of the great people who worked there such as Jimmy Burns, Ed Danforth, Tarleton Collier, Tom Ripley, Randy Edmondson, Tobe Edwards, Ed Miles, Charley Shonesy, O.B. Keeler, and a copy boy named Catfish. When I was a contributing sports editor I would submit my copy and if they did publish it, it was my duty to read the paper, cut out my stuff, paste it together in what they termed a string and turn it in for which I would receive the magnificent sum of twenty-five cents per column inch.

RAILROAD MEMORIES

What a thrill it was as a boy to ride on the train. My train rides were mainly to say Warm Springs to a Sunday School outing or to Covington to see kin folks. Trains left principally in Atlanta from the Terminal Station or the Union Station. Both were in downtown Atlanta. Before departure a "train caller" would come out with a megaphone and say something like this: "Train Number 37 for East Point, College Park, Hapeville, Griffin, Barnesville, Forsyth, Macon, and other points south now at Track 21, departing in ten minutes, BOOAARRD." He was my hero. What a great life I thought it would be if you could grow up to be the train caller at the terminal station. That same fellow used to shop at the grocery store where I worked on Fridays and Saturdays and when he came in we all felt that some class of royalty had visited us.

There was no air conditioning. The whistle which was blown for all the numerous crossings made a thrilling, exciting sound and I can hear it even now. The seats were sticky red or green plush. I have never known how all the cinders got into the seating area but they were there right on. There was an observation car at the back end of the train and you could stand or sit out there. You could not tell where you were headed but you surely could see where you had been. That too was a great experience. Then when you passed another train going in the opposite direction it shocked and scared you at first for you had no idea it was coming. Those were the days when men wore hats. Seasoned travelers such as "traveling men" always stuck their ticket stubs in the band around their hat brim. They were old and experienced hands at the game. It was fun but those days are gone. They now have drawing rooms, upper and lower berths, roomettes, air conditioning, no cinders, and dining cars in abundance.

⟋⟍

THINGS WE USED TO DO BUT DON'T SEE NOW

Things there are that in my early years were much in vogue among us barefooted kids and I see no evidence of their being done today. These are the things I am talking about: shooting marbles, spinning tops, walking on homemade stilts, playing catch where two of you threw the ball back and forth to each other out in the yard, making mud pies, sneaking off and smoking rabbit tobacco, cornsilk, or cubebs, climbing trees (we would climb some high ones), shooting BB guns, playing hide and seek and hop-scotch, taking an old worn out car, stripping it of its main outside body and creating yourself what we called a "cut down," getting a job in the summer "jerking soda" at the corner drug store, operating a curb-side "drink stand" where all soft drinks sold for a nickel, and lots of other things.

And I never hear used now the term, "I double-dog dare you to do this or that." Daring one to do something was much milder than double-dog daring another. Another game you no longer see is mumbly peg, a game you played with pocket knives the details of which are too lengthy and complicated to set out here. Corner me sometime and I will give you a lesson in mumbly peg. Of course, such games as "spin the bottle" and activities like "prom parties" came much later in our teen years. The first time I ever took a girl to a party (it was a birthday party in the mid-afternoon), my mama gave me detailed instructions on where to walk when walking with her (always with me nearest the street), to say, "Thank you ma'am" and, "No thank you," instead of, "OK, thanks" and, "Naw, I don't want any." It was over finally and was I glad. But I had to give an honest accounting of what had taken place where I was involved at the party. The girl's name was May Padgett and she lived just a block away from our house. She was a pretty 11 year old little lady, too.

SANDLOT BASEBALL YEARS AGO

Between the ages of 8 and 12 we used to play sandlot baseball. Not having enough players to have two teams we played what we called "rotation." It was every man for himself. If it was your turn at bat, you tried to hit the ball, run to the only base (which was usually a big rock) and then back home before they could get the ball and tag you out. You kept on batting until you got put out. Then another took your place at bat.

Some little runt guy always got to play because he owned the only ball and if he was not allowed to play, he would go home and take his ball with him. The balls were by no means standard balls, but cheap ones. Frequently the covers would come off and we would hold them together by putting black tire-tape all around what was left of the ball. It became heavy and not exactly round but we didn't mind too much.

Pitching at that tender age was all underhanded. It was sort of standard procedure when some guy knocked a rather high fly or foul that when the fielder was trying to catch it we would yell, "Bicycle!" meaning, look out, somebody left his bicycle there and you are about to stumble on it. He would look down and lose eye contact with the ball and usually miss it. Seldom was a bicycle there but we yelled, "bicycle" every time anyway.

To decide who batted first, a bat would be tossed. One guy would catch it in his hand grip, then the next guy would grip above it with his hand and when you got to the top the last guy who gripped it (and it was usually with thumb and one finger) he had to be able to swing it around his head and toss it ten feet without dropping it. If he could, he was first batter. Those were great days.

PLAYING MARBLES FOR KEEPS

Also we played a lot of marbles when I was a jay bird. Our marbles were as follows: (a) The most treasured was an agate; (b) Next was a cornelian which had wavy marks on it and was in most cases reddish brown in color; (c) Third was the "frenchy" which was a standard basic marble; and (d) Finally there was the "doggie" or "twosy" as they were called. They were looked down on and were not in demand. They were made of clay. A ring made by drawing two semicircular lines in the dirt with their ends crossing was the playing area. Each player put in a marble.

Shooting taw was a line drawn some ten feet from the ring behind which each player would (taking turns) shoot his shooting marble, usually called also his "taw," toward the ring where the marbles had been placed. All marbles you were able to knock out of the ring with your taw, you could keep. This was playing for "keeps." In shooting you had to have your "knucks," as we all called our knuckles, down on the ground. When all marbles had been knocked from the ring, the game was over and another would start. Some of those guys were really good. One guy named Miller Kirk was a whiz. He was so good we would hardly let him in our average games. I ended up with literally sacks full of marbles, some won in games and others traded for. 'Twas great fun but I doubt if anything like that is now played by the current day youngsters.

BOYS IN COMPETITION WITH EACH OTHER

As grammar school pupils I and the other boys in the classes had things we yearned for and things as to which we sought to outdo each other. If you could do something another could not do you "cacked" him. I guess that is the way to spell cack. Something like jumping over a barbed wire fence without being scratched or mangled. Then there were certain things as to which we always wanted to compare ourselves to the others in the age group. For instance, I always wanted to be tall. Also, I yearned for the day when I would weigh 100 pounds. Another thing was chinning. Chinning was the ability to reach up to an acting bar and hold on to it with both hands, palms back toward your face and pull yourself up so that your chin would go over the height of the acting bar. One time was not too hard but to do ten chin-ups without touching the ground was tough, at least for me. I guess all boys want to grow tall and attain some physical prowess. If I recall it I was about in the eighth grade when I attained 100 pounds in weight. Now it is reversed, I want to lose weight. I could chin all right but was by no means the champion chinner. I eventually attained the height of 6 feet 1 inch and the strange thing to me is that I attained all my height by the time I was fifteen years old and in high school. I am sure the girls of that age had things they sought to attain but no one of them ever confided in me as to what they were and I still don't know. Maybe it was to have curly hair or some such thing as that but I never knew. Girls just did not interest me in those years and I am positive that it worked both ways and that I never interested the girls.

The whole approach changes as you get old and full of years. In fact, I heard two men talking the other day and one said to the other, "Can you still take a tub bath and get out of the tub without assistance?" The one asking the question could not. The other one said he still could and both were in advanced years. Therefore, the one who still could perform that feat had at considerable age "cacked" the other. Times do change and the view from the top of the hill is definitely different from that at the bottom.

4

Those Were the Days

There were swings on people's front porches in which they sat and swung back and forth with the swing making a characteristic squeaking noise and no one ever seemed to take the trouble to oil it. I think the reason was that they liked the squeak. It was a homey sound. You could tell the Joneses' swing sound from the Whites'. There were also on most porches banisters on which at least the men in the family liked to prop their feet. The chairs were always rocking chairs usually with cane bottoms and in most of them there was some sort of pillow. Sofas were then called settees and were in those days really not too comfortable. But then came the overstuffed sofas and they were "in."

I like sofas. On them you can take a nap, read the paper and put the part just finished right there beside you and do lots of other things. Children particularly like them for the reason they can run and jump up on them in play. Don't knock sofas and also these reclining chairs. What a joy they are in which to nap.

CORSETS AND OTHER-SUCH STUFF

Was talking to a lady recently and she was recalling the days when she was young and how her mother and all the ladies wore tight fitting and very confining corsets. A corset was a sort of a wrap around body piece that went from the breast to the pelvis and was smaller in the middle than at either end. It was tightly laced, pulled in at the middle to give the impression of a much smaller waist than was actually the case. It was stiffened with "stays" made usually of whalebone which was flexible and resumed its normal straightness when the corset was removed. Fitters would, when asked to do so, come to the home of the person buying the corset and fit it. Many were pink and had snaps on the lower end to use to hold up the silk stockings usually worn when the corset was. What a burden that must have been to wear and what a relief the modern woman must feel at no longer being expected by style to use any such clothing.

But there is another odd thing about the apparel of men and women that I recently noted. Increasingly the ladies are wearing hats to church and they are usually attractive. No voice is raised against it but were a man to wear his hat to church it would be considered in extreme bad taste and to a degree that it would be almost sacrilegious. Do you recall way back when butchers in meat markets wore straw hat?. I worked in a store where such was the case and the butcher told me they did not like to be referred to as butchers but by the more respected title "meat cutters." Butchers he said usually killed the animal while the meat cutters dealt much more delicately with it as they from the carcass sliced and trimmed the cuts desired by the lady shoppers such as ham, veal cutlets, round steak, pork ribs, pork chops, lamb chops, porterhouse steaks and the like.

THE SAFE

In nearly every home when I was growing up there was a cabinet, usually the highest in the kitchen or nearby, in which the housewife kept her china, glassware and other such household standbys. We always called it "the safe" at our house. Mama would say, "Son, go put the glass back in the safe." She never referred to it as a cabinet. I wonder if that was a term used in most of the households or whether we alone used it.

WHAT THE LADS AND LASSES LOOKED FORWARD TO IN THEIR YOUTH

Some of the things I cherished and looked forward to when I was a lad were:

(a) When I would be allowed to wear long pants instead of knee britches.

(b) When I would weigh 100 pounds.

(c) When I could ride a bicycle.

(d) First time I would be allowed to wear a suit and tie.

(e) My first real unchaperoned date.

(f) My first time kissing a girl.

(g) My first real money-earning job.

(h) My high school graduation.

I had no idea what the girls looked forward to so I had to ask around to a number of them to get a kind of agreement as to what they were and the following came up as proper to be on a girl's list:

(a) First time allowed to wear silk stockings.

(b) First pair of high heel shoes.

(c) First time allowed to put makeup on face, etc.

(d) First unchaperoned date.

(e) First time to kiss a boy.

(f) First long dress and permanent wave.

(g) Some other more personal things.

POUND THE PREACHER

Back in the olden days in the Methodist Church the preachers were moved to a new church about every four years so as to let the congregations share the bad ones as well as the good. It was the custom when the new preacher arrived for the members of the congregation to "pound the preacher," i.e. every member would bring to him at his residence, called the parsonage, a pound of some food since he had not had a chance to provide these since he came. They would not of course limit the amount to a pound but would bring eggs, butter, salt, pepper, ham, sugar, pork chops, steak, soap, and all of the things a household needed. Sounds like a good practice to me and I guess some ministers wish it could be revived as a custom.

OLD STREET CARS

Way back in the 1920's the street railway system in Atlanta was owned and operated by the Georgia Power and Electric Company. The cars were powered by electricity and ran on tracks situated in the middle of the streets on which they had established routes. Each car had a two man crew. The motorman rode in front and handled the controls to run the car. The conductor rode in the back and, since all passengers entered by the back door and exited by the front door, it was the conductor who collected fares. To begin with they were five cents but went up to 7 cents later and even higher. When the last waiting customer had been allowed aboard and paid his or her fare, the conductor pulled a cord which rang two bells in the motorman's quarters as a message to "let's go." From those bells the company named its little paper placed in racks by each seat Two Bells. Signs were prominently placed which read, "Colored will seat from the rear toward front" and, "Whites will seat from front toward rear." There was no upholstery on the seats and at the end of the line the conductor would walk down the aisle turning the seat backs so passengers on return trip would sit facing forward. If you wished to get off at the next stop you reached overhead and pulled a cord that rang another bell at the motorman's side and he stopped at the next stop to let you off. There was a big trolley over the car which ran along a charged electric cable providing the power. At the end of the run the motorman got off and, by an attached rope, turned the overhead trolley around for the return trip. There were straps hanging from the roof of the car inside to enable standers to hold on to these straps and not fall. Thus came the term "strap hangers." I always as a kid wanted to grow up to become a street car motorman.

I would have loved it and am even now disappointed a bit. The cars were painted green and some yellow on them as I recall it. I think the biggest civic mistake made in Atlanta during my lifetime is the abandonment of the Marietta and Stone Mountain rights-of-way on which MARTA could now carry passengers to those destinations.

MAKING MONEY IN THE OLD DAYS

I have noticed how many young persons today talk so fast that we "mature" locals cannot understand them. They also mumble. Their jargon also does not help the situation. At a parking garage today the attendant gave me a ticket and said something I could not understand. I finally decided that what he was saying was simply — you get out — leave the keys and I will park it for you. At the rates they charged ($3 for less than 2 hours) I felt he should have washed it as well. It made me think of the times when I was in high school and went to Fort Valley, Georgia, each summer to work in peaches. I got the magnificent pay of 20 cents per hour for an 8-hour day coming to a total of $1.60 per diem and I was glad to get it and needed the job. Peach fuzz was in good supply and it kept us busy scratching all day long. Them was the days.

And that reminds me that our first maid was paid $3.50 per week, and I am not now sure she was worth it. But then Coca-Colas and wieners were five cents each and it cost ten cents to go to the picture show. I am not recommending it but simply recalling it.

MORE ABOUT GROCERY STORES

As a high schooler I had a job Friday afternoons and Saturdays working in an A&P Store. It was not self-service. Clerks waited on customers. The customer stated her needs and the clerk went and got it. She might ask for a box of Nucoa, or a pound of sugar or lard, or a pound of coffee (ground for a percolator, please). I remember one lady who came every Saturday and the store manager insisted he wait on her because he told me that she would spend some Saturdays as much as ten dollars. Men would come in to buy chewing tobacco. They would ask for a hair plug of Brown's Mule, Schnapps, or Apple Sun Cures. I became sort of an expert at cutting these pieces for them. Cheese was on a big round wheel and was 32 cents a pound. I would turn the wheel and then with the big cutter attached slice what I felt was the amount she ordered.

One manager told me on a Saturday to go into the back and sack up pounds of sugar so when the ladies asked for it we would have it ready. I was doing just this when he came to me and said put only 15 ounces in each sack. I said that was not a pound. He said he knew it but he took losses on vegetables that spoiled and he had to make up for that somewhere. I told him I would put 15 ounces to a sack if he would mark it 15 ounces but if he was gonna mark it one pound, I was gonna put 16 ounces in. His response was, "Boy, you ain't never gonna make manager." I never did either.

They cleaned out the windows each Saturday night at closing and I would decorate the windows for over the weekend observers. I arranged cereal boxes and other things in what I considered attractive arrangements but it was basically corny.

The meat market was in the back of the store. The butcher cut the meat to order from a big side of meat he kept in the refrigerator. When steak was ordered for instance I can now hear the butcher Mr. Hickman in response to some lady's inquiry, "Mr. Hickman, is this meat fresh?" and he would lean far over the counter and say, "Mrs. Hackenbush, this meat is so fresh, I have had to call it down twice this morning already." We sold stick matches. We sold kerosene by the gallon. Customers would bring cans with a spout on them and they always seemed to stick an Irish potato on the spout to keep it from spilling out as they trudged homeward. All candy bars were a nickel.

~

NOSTALGIC EXPRESSIONS AND THOUGHTS

Everybody used to know what was meant by the term "kindling wood" but now a teenager would not know what you were talking about. It was the smaller, shorter pieces of dry wood you would put at the bottom of the grate and on top of which you would pile logs. The smaller wood burned easier and kindled the logs. There were also what was known as "lighter knots" and these were odd shaped pieces of pine, small size, but loaded with resin and would light their pipe or cigar. The term "white as a sheet" used to be expressive but now that sheets are blue, pink, and all sorts of other colors it is not as clearly meaningful as it once was.

~

NO MORE BLOTTERS

I would hate to be in the blotter business. Ball points have put them out of business. You used to get them as advertisements in such places as funeral homes, insurance agencies and banks, but no more. Ran across some in the bottom of an old dresser drawer the other day and was amused at seeing them.

~

SAD MEMORIES

I recall in my youth they had at the Fulton County Jailhouse what was called the Fulton Tower. It was constructed of granite and was a small circular structure adjoining the jailhouse. It was in this Fulton Tower that the hanging of criminals who had been sentenced to death was carried out. There of course was a scaffold and the usual trap that was sprung allowing the condemned person to fall through and be hanged "until death do come." I also recall riding along through the country with my parents and seeing the prisoner work gangs at work. The standard attire was a suit of sort of coveralls made of black and white striped cloth.

Also attached to each of the prisoners working on the roads was a heavy metal ball probably weighing 10 to 20 pounds. These were shackled to the prisoner so he could not run. These prisoner work groups were known as chain gangs. Fortunately electrocution has replaced the old hanging method and they no longer use the stripes and the ball and chain. Just before each hanging a black face and head mask was placed entirely over the head and face of the person to be executed. When the coroner or some other designated person certified that the hanged person was dead his body was taken down and turned over to his family to be buried and if no one claimed the body, it was buried in the county graveyard. We have made some progress at any rate in the treatment we humans give each other.

HATS

Have you noticed how hats for both men and women have sort of passed from the scene? I used to wear a regular snap-brimmed hat (Stetson they called it) regularly. My daddy wore a hat every day. This is no longer the case. I still have the old hats but seldom wear one. Caps have taken over and lots of them are in view. Arafat still wears that towel on his head. The Turks wear fezzes and the Arabs wear turbans. I sort of liked hats, tell you the truth, and I hate to see them now passing out of style. Men used to wear derby hats, and some wore fuzzy fedoras as we called them.

As a lad I wore a skull cap the colors of my grammar school which were red and green. I recall one day going in a tad late to law school, removing my gray felt hat and slapping it on the head of the bust of Judge John S. Candler which was in the lobby and for this infraction I was that day called to the office of the dean to be remonstrated with in a rather serious fashion for a lack of proper decorum. Ladies too used to wear hats. My mama did. Some of them had feathers and even red cherries adorning them. Nevertheless, I did on this last Easter count about ten ladies with hats on at our church. About five of these were preteen or teenage girls. Somehow in lots of these cases the hats were becoming to the ladies and I sort of hate to see them now going by the board.

＊

NOSTALGIC DRIVE

Went to Decatur the other night to meet friends for dinner and chose to go on Peachtree to Ponce de Leon and then on into Decatur. That is the most direct route. I drove along slowly and I passed many, many points that had figured in my life and that I was impressed by. I had a real nostalgic feeling. Among the places passed were the First Presbyterian Church where I was married in 1937; the old Biltmore Hotel in which I played as a boy while it was a-building; then onto Ponce de Leon and Grace Methodist Church where Charlie Allen was so long the pastor and for whom I served as attorney on occasion; then to Jackson Street down at the bottom of which Boys' High School was located, which I attended from 1925-1928; then on by what was Spiller's Park where the Atlanta Crackers played Southern League baseball and in which I at various times sold Coca-Colas and peanuts and kept the scoreboard (nonelectronic) for which I was paid $2 per game. (Don't knock it, that was good money.) I also passed the first drive-in site in Atlanta, called The Pig and Whistle. And on out Ponce de Leon by St. Charles Avenue where my wife Ellen was born, and thence by the old A&P Store where I clerked while in high school on Saturdays. I then passed Druid Hills Methodist Church where I joined the church in about 1920 and then on by the former home of Asa Candler and also that of Henry Heinz who was murdered there during the war years; and on past Druid Hills Golf Club where our wedding reception was held in 1937. On into the next block where at 1766 Ponce de Leon, Ellen's folks lived and where I courted her for some six years prior to our marriage. We later moved into that home after her mother's death in 1938 and lived there for 12 years. Then on to Decatur where I have tried some interesting cases in the old DeKalb County Courthouse. Yep, it rekindled a lot of fires and brought back myriad memories of earlier and more vigorous years. Memory is a great thing if you can restrict it to memories of the good and not the bad things that have happened. Fortunately for me the good have far outweighed and outnumbered the bad so it was a pleasant ride and a wonderful experience.

~

PROHIBITION DAYS

Back in the 1920's when prohibition was in full flower and speakeasies were the vogue, lots of funny things happened. Our mayor then was James L. Key. He made a trip of some sort to Paris. A picture was sent home to the press of him being in some restaurant like the Cafe De La Paix or some other bistro. On the table was a bottle of wine. The city was shocked. The press and the preachers had a heyday. He was excoriated and almost pilloried. He had a rough time of it. How times have changed.

~

ICE

How well I remember when the first refrigerator that made its own ice came to our neighborhood. It was in the 1920's I believe it was. The machine was owned by the parents of my friend Tom Clark. They lived on Seminole Avenue, not too far from my house.

We all marveled at this great departure. Ice in those days, though a treasured thing, had to be purchased daily from the "ice man" who came by in a horse-drawn wagon or a truck with cakes of ice stored in it. You would tell him how much (in weight) you wished and he, with a really sharp ice-pick, would cut off that much. The ice blocks had indentations on them to show where one would cut for the different weights.

Once having cut the chunk for the housewife, he would cover it with a croker sack (burlap bag to you) and lift it onto his shoulder and carry it into the house and deposit it in the ice box. Usually ice was placed in the top part of the ice box so it could drip into a water pan below the ice box which would have to be emptied daily at least once.

In chipping the ice sometimes the ice man would break off a piece which all of us kids would joyfully take over, place it on the sidewalk and crack it and eat it right there, germs to the contrary notwithstanding. The ice wagon had a sign on its side which read, "Atlantic Ice and Coal Company."

FOODS THEN AND NOW

All of us I am certain look back on our childhood with some nostalgic affection. A good bit of it grows out of the family dinner table. The foods Mama prepared. Daddy's blessings. The relaxed and unhurried approach to the evening meal. It occurred to me that many changes have been now made and children probably don't get the same old feelings we had. At our house, the regular standard vegetables were turnip greens, Irish potatoes, sweet potatoes, squash, black-eyed peas, string beans, carrots, baked beans, beets, butter beans, and a few others. We never ever heard of parsley, water cress, Brussels sprouts, zucchini, and many of the other exotic and different vegetables now served regularly. Also, we had biscuits, corn bread, sometimes rolls and for sandwiches we used what was then termed "light bread," which is the same as our current loaf bread. We had never heard of croissants, bagels, pizza, and English muffins. In England, I once asked for an English muffin. They didn't know what I was talking about. Breads were white, whole wheat, and rye. Some families of what we felt were of foreign extraction ate "pumpernickel," which we felt was a funny name for an ugly bread.

Our meats were pork, beef, lamb, chicken and on occasion liver. I recall Mama used to make Irish potato and sweet potato croquettes. Man alive, but they were good. They were just as sweet and as tender as my heart. I wish I had some right now.

Talking about Daddy saying the blessing, he had a rather fun-loving brother who was a sort of cutup. Daddy at one meal said, "Ralph, will you say the blessing?" Whereupon Uncle Ralph and the others bowed their heads and my unorthodox uncle intoned, "Eat the meat, leave the skin, back your ears and poke it in." My straightlaced daddy never made that mistake again.

5

Peculiarities of People

I looked at the ground in my backyard the other day and I saw a bunch of ants walking along in a row. Some were going this way and some the other way. I wondered why they weren't all going in the same direction if it was for food they sought. But then I am by no means an expert on ants and decided just to leave all that to them. They know more about ant-doings than I will ever know.

Two days later I was looking down from my office window on the 25th floor of the building much in the same manner and I saw many, many automobiles similarly in lines or rows, and some were headed this way and yet others in equally long lines were traveling in the opposite direction and even crosswise from the other two streams. It reminded me of the ants and I figured that if all these auto drivers knew why and where they were going, the ants in all likelihood similarly knew why they were doing what they were doing.

So I just decided not to bother my pointed head about such matters anymore and to leave both ants and automobile drivers to their own devices.

IN THE WAITING ROOM

I visited the eye doctor the other day. Got to watching others there. Nearly everybody who goes to the doctor is on pins and needles about the visit. I guess they figure he is gonna find the person has some dread disease or will have to face surgery or be put in a wheelchair or something. Other patients were reading magazines — or made out like they were — two had the magazines upside down. Another was sitting stiff-backed on the edge of the chair anxiously concerned. One was alternately crossing his legs. Seems like one crossing would be enough. Another was sitting ramrod straight in utter anxiety and still another kept jiggling his foot up and down continuously. I just sit there and watch, for under my newly adopted philosophy nothing bothers me anymore.

At the doctor's office, I relax and say to myself, "Boy, you either got it or you ain't got it. And if you ain't got it, you have nothing to worry about and if you have got it, you are at the right place and the doctor has your best interest at heart and will do all he can to cure it, whatever it is." I adopted this philosophy for the simple reason that either way there is nothing I can do that I am not already doing. It is a great idea if you can adopt it. Not all can. Try it.

CUBANS FED UP WITH RUSSIA

Once while Ellen and I were in Moscow, we went to the Bolshoi Ballet. They were performing Swan Lake as I recall it, but that is not important. We could not get seats together so I was way to the right and she was way to the left in a vast ballet hall. I was near the wall and two persons occupied seats by me. I hated to turn and stare at them since they might be prime Bolsheviks, so I just sat and listened, awaiting the rise of the curtain. I heard their talk and decided they were not speaking Russian, nor was it English.

I decided to "white eye" them, that is, to face forward but to let my eyes turn as far to the right as possible so I could see them better. As I did I found the guy on my right was "white eyeing" me. So I spoke and they were from Cuba and were speaking Spanish. Since I as a C student had taken Spanish in high school, I talked a bit with them in my fluent Spanish and learned they were from Havana, Cuba, and had known my old friend in Atlanta, Elliott Haas, for many years, since he married an Havana girl and visited there frequently.

They had already found themselves fully saturated with Russia and were going home and wreak great punishment on the travel agent who had booked them into the Soviet Union for a week. They were already fed up.

SOME GUYS JUST HAVE TO GET INTO THE ACT

Have you ever noticed that in nearly every public gathering, seminar, or some such conference, there is some guy who repeatedly speaks up, asks questions in a profound voice which generally are not questions but "answers" which he is prepared to give if someone would but ask the proper question. The first such outburst is generally well received but as it is repeated again and again, the crowd catches on (i.e. all but the guy doing the talking) and they patiently wait through it all until he has exhausted his "advice to the group" and the meeting can go on again minus his "advice." These folks somehow never seem to see themselves as everybody else sees them. It takes all kinds, you know.

SOME CAN AND SOME CAN'T

Pretty hard to determine what it is that makes some folks good at what they do and others with equal education and basic intelligence just plain unable to come across. This is certainly true of preachers. Some could preach on the Sermon on the Mount and you would go to sleep while others could recite the begats and you could hardly wait to see who next begat whom. Maybe it is the twinkle in the eye, the inflection of the voice, the sly smile or grimace that flits in and out. The same is true about lawyers.

All have been admitted to the bar but some could know all of corpus juris by heart and not be able to win a case in the traffic court whereas others don't know a fee simple from a femme sole and can't lose. I am sure the doctors probably see this in their profession as well as others in theirs. Anyone who could identify and come up with the secret of why this is could certainly make a fortune. Some may call it for want of a better term "personality" but again personality is not easily defined. Whatever it is, if it ever goes on sale I plan to be there when the store opens.

IDENTIFYING IN THE SOUTH

Somehow down here in the South we seem to put much more store on identifying with others than they apparently do elsewhere in the country. For instance, I was at the courthouse today and one of the fine lady clerks whom I had worked with for years said to me she had seen me once down in Meriwether County where my small farm is located. She asked if I had any connections there. I told her my grandpa came from one of the smaller rural communities in Meriwether County. She to my great surprise said that her folks too had come from that county. Her maiden name she said was Rowe. This fact sort of changed our relationship. We had always gotten along well but now that we both have ties to the same county, we feel closer and we have an identifying relationship that gives added depth to our understanding and appreciation of each other. In fact, the county agent in Meriwether if I recall correctly is named Rowe and I bet he is kin to her too. I am gonna ask her next time I am in her office. If somebody's daddy knew my daddy or if somebody's mama and my mama were in the same class at college this identifies me with them in a deeper way than otherwise. I hope this takes place in other sections of the nation. I don't really know but I do know it is a real fact of life here in the South and I love it. All of us like to be "identified" with others. It is just human nature I guess.

RECEPTIONS, PARTIES AND LADIES ATTIRE

Went recently to a reception given at a club for a newly married couple which was from 5 until 7 in the late afternoon. All the men had on attire that were standards. They wore suits, ties, conservative accessories and were generally uniform in appearance. But, man, you should have seen the ladies. They had on a varied array of attire. Some had dresses down to their ankles. Others had on skirts up to here. Some were more or less tastefully dressed and others had on weirdo stuff such as britches or long pants or slacks whatever they call them. Some had on short little skirts with black stuff all down to their shoes that looked like black long underwear. They were so skinny they looked sort of like spiders to me. Come to think about it the ladies must have some real problems when deciding what to wear to a gathering. Shall I wear my long dress down to my ankles or my short dress up to here? Or shall I wear my long britches or my spider outfit? One thing is for sure, if you want to be spotted easily at a get-together, wear your red dress. They are easy to locate. Then there is yet another thing at these parties. Someone will come up to you and say, "I am so glad to see you. This is Naomi, Jerome's wife." You are glad to get to meet old Naomi of course, but who in the heck is Jerome?

EVERYBODY WANTS A JOB

All of my life I have attended Sunday School and I still do. We have a great class called the Fellowship Class at Northside Methodist Church. There are some 75 to 100 members and our weekly attendance is about 60. But I have noticed that there is a sort of pattern in Sunday School classes that I have been fortunate enough to attend. Some guy becomes the self-appointed janitor. He regulates the air conditioning and heating, opens and closes blinds and checks on all electrically operated devices such as lights and loud speakers. Then there is a guy who hands out and collects at the end of the service the song books and stores them appropriately. There are chair arrangers and flower ladies who make sure flowers are on hand each Sunday. Then too there are those ladies who make and bring cookies and cakes for the coffee hour. All of these folks are important and necessary adjuncts to the class operation, but it is amazing how many of them are self-appointed. The class couldn't operate nearly so well without these folks but what is remarkable to me is that there is a sort of fixed pattern on self-appointed officials in every class I have ever belonged to. I guess some folks just have a janitorial complex.

NEW THINGS I HAVE SEEN

There is seemingly always some new fad taking on. I have noticed recently that both men and women when going about have begun to wear a sort of pouch around the waist in which they store something. It hangs in front of the person and what they put in it I don't know. It seems it would be dangerous to carry your money in it and it is not usually large enough to hold anything bulky but they have come into pretty wide use I have noticed among travelers. I saw it in Washington on a short trip there in May.

By the way one of the attractive things about D.C. is that there are so many wide-open grassy plots about like meadows at various points about the area. Folks lunch there, relax and just seem to revel in the open air and warm wide open spaces. I wish we had such in Atlanta but they have all become filling stations, shopping malls, and parking lots it seems. In D.C. there also seem to be many more long, black stretch limousines with dark tinted windows so that you cannot see who is riding in them. I have always felt I would like to ride in one but guess I never will. I get the feeling that due to the dark glass there must be some Indian Rajah or other dignitary inside who wishes to travel incognito. But on the other hand it may be some jerk from Opp, Alabama, just putting on the dog.

COUNTRY FAIRS

Country fairs have come into vogue again. They are usually held in some place of easy access, on relatively level ground, with ample parking available for all and generally at some crossroads location where folks can get to them from all four directions. One such fair is held at Gay, Georgia, (unfortunate name) near where my farm is. It is held on the first weekend in May and October and is exceptionally well attended with over 200 exhibitors. Mary Lamar and I went this year with a friend of hers. It was amazing. I never saw so many fat folks in my life. The fat ones were predominantly women and they waddled and lurched all over the place. Paintings, jewelry, homemade wooden items, balloons, barbecue, boiled peanuts, leather goods, quilts, dolls, aprons, T-shirts, candy and everything else imaginable was for sale. If you have not been to one let me urge you to go this coming May. Ask me and I will tell you how to get there.

And talking about fat folks, there were plenty of fat men too — some in overalls and others in coveralls. So many men, and especially the fat ones, seem to wear their belts below their paunch, and so far down it is amazing that their britches don't fall down. That reminds me of a cook we once had who was heavy and short. My wife Ellen took her somewhere to see an event from the stands. Ellen asked her if being so short she needed a pillow in order to see, and her reply was, "No, ma'am, Miss Ellen, I can see all right, I jes sits high-rumpted."

<hr>

SOME "FRIENDS" SEEM ALWAYS TO WANT SOMETHING

When you get a phone call from some old friend usually it is welcome for they want you to eat lunch or go to dinner with them. Usually you go and are flattered that you have been called. You enjoy the outing and wish it happened much more frequently. But then there are some "friends" who, when they call (and thank goodness it is rare that they call), you know there is something they want from you or want you to do for them or something like that. They start in with the usual chitchat and then along about the second cup of coffee they let it all out. They say, "By the way, would you mind seeing what you can do about getting my sister's niece a job at the pickle works? I know you know the manager down there. You do remember my sister Xenophia, I am sure.

Well, this is her husband's brother's daughter and she lives in Outhouse, Arkansas, and she just loves pickles. I am sure she would fit in perfectly. She plans to be here for three days next week and I told Xenophia that I was sure you would do anything you can to help. Shall I bring her to your office or to your house when she gets here?"

Of course, you only know the head man at the pickle works because you and he were next to each other in the checkout line at the Piggly Wiggly grocery store one time recently. But to your friend that makes you a close buddy of the guy. You want to help anyone you can, but this sort of "friend" seems always to have something in mind that he wants from you instead of just your company and that makes you leery and reserved when such a friend calls.

GRABBING HOLD OF YOU

Ever notice how some folks when they talk to you reach over and hold on to you or grab your arm, or punch you in the chest. I have two or three close friends who do this. It doesn't exactly appeal to me. I can get what they are saying without being grabbed or punched or held on to. Just say it. Don't squeeze it. I guess it is for the purpose of showing closeness and that is good, but to do such with every statement made seems to me to be a bit too much. If what they are saying has a punch line, let the line do the punching and not the person. Them's my sentiments.

ELEVATOR HABITS

Ever notice what folks do when they ride an elevator? The person steps into the elevator and if you are going down on the elevator and the person already on the elevator has punched the button designated "lobby," the new arrival, even though he sees button already lighted, will almost invariably punch it again as if to say to the electronic device, "I want to go to the lobby, too, so count me in." The same thing applies if people going up see that the floor to which they are headed has already been punched. They punch it again, saying, "I, too, want to go to that floor." Then, if the elevator walls are mirrored, the ladies seem always to walk in and adjust their skirts, collars, hair, and the like while the men just stare and often look up at the ceiling or down at the floor.

If before the elevator closes the door to start on its journey it seems to become jerky and the door opens and shuts and opens again then sort of shudders, lots of the passengers, for fear it may be broken and may fall, hastily make their exits to safety. Can't much blame folks for this attitude. Sometimes also elevators get stuck between floors for hours.

Escalators are another thing. Many older people find them hazardous since their movement is not geared to the agility of the senior citizen and, in lots of instances, they elect to ride the elevators instead. My mama was that way and I knew one young person who had some sort of a phobia and would not ride an escalator. Though I may live to regret it some day, I nevertheless ride them all up and down and enjoy the ride while it lasts.

6

Emory

Some folks have asked me from time to time why I have such a devotion to my alma mater Emory University. So I decided to try and answer that question. Among many others, these are some of the reasons:

(a) She provided both my father and me with what I refer to as a basically excellent college education at a cost which now seems ridiculous but which then was the going rate. Tuition was $25 per month ($75 per quarter). Total cost for college and law school was $1,350. (I paid $1,800 tuition for one year for my grandson in play school.)

(b) It created an interest in books and learning which had not previously existed in me.

(c) It put me in touch closely with learned faculty members whose ideals and philosophies have stayed with me.

(d) It was in a Christ centered religious setting.

(e) It provided me with an opportunity to participate in athletics and physical training at a level of my own abilities which may not be so readily available at highly athletic-oriented universities.

(f) It provided me with a working knowledge in my profession to which I have devoted the major portion of my life, with pleasure and profit.

(g) It has provided me also with a real host of wonderful friends with whom the friendship there begun has continued over the intervening 61 years or so. This has been listed last but it is by no means last in importance. I just shudder to think what life would be without good, loyal and devoted friends. I have as I see it had far greater blessings in this area than I was or am entitled to, and to Emory University for that alone I will be forever grateful.

The above is not an exhaustive list but certainly a good beginning and am sure that many other folks could add significantly to it as I know they will.

A MEMORABLE(?) RHYME

While a student at Emory in the twenties and thirties, composed this, so please forgive me.

Back in '36 when Emory first began,
The total enrollment was just one man,
When up jumped a guy named Ignatius A. Few
And said listen here fellow, tell you what let's do.
Down at little Oxford we'll start us up a college,
And arrange for most of us to get a bit of knowledge.
We'll name it for our bishop whose last name is Emory.
And that's the way it started to the best of my information,
The very finest university in all our nation.

MEMORIES OF EMORY

Next to my family and my church I am sure that Emory University has had more of an influence on me and has served a greater degree of satisfaction to me than any other thing with which I have had a close connection. I entered in the fall of 1928 and finished both college and law school in August of 1933 by going to several summer schools. Inspiration, fair dealing, the closest of friends, and better understanding of human beings are among the many benefits which came to me. I don't know about others but those of us who shared a stay at Emory together in those years named have retained a closeness which to me seems unique. This week for instance, I had a dinner Monday night with an old Emory friend from Alabama, dinner on Thursday night with three others, lunch today with another, dinner tonight with yet one more and it goes on and on just like that. I am sure others have experienced continued friendships, but I am talking only about what happened to me due to my having gone to Emory and for it I am deeply and continually grateful.

Even though we did not have intercollegiate athletics at Emory, we did have some yells of which the following are two: "Emory, Emory, ain't we hell, Candler, Byfield, Debouchelle." (I will have to explain to any interested ones the significance of some of the names.) Then there was another and it went this way:

Emory, Emory, thy future we foretell,
We were raised on Coca-Cola
So no wonder we raise hell.
When we meet Tech's engineers
We will drink them off their stools,
So raise a cup and here's to the luck
Of the Coca-Cola school.

VICTORY

When I was at Emory and there was a conflict between class or football, you immediately went to class. My late friend Pollard (Booshie) Turman was a great football player and a fine student. He went to class instead of football one day but got out of class about halfway through the game. He went to his locker, dressed out, and ran onto the field to join his team. Bruce Logue, another of our friends, told me he saw Boosh coming and said to him, "Now maybe we can get going." Well, Boosh got into the game and on about the third or fourth play, lay way out to the side,

Bruce tossed him a ball and he went straight down the sidelines for a victory. Emory's athletics got very little attention in the press but, nevertheless, there was a great admiration for the stars by those who were there. What I just related was told to me only last week by our mutual friend Dr. Bruce Logue who has remembered this for over fifty years. "Bravissimo."

7

Folks I Have Known

Bishop Arthur Moore was, at one time, the Bishop for the area that included the Congo in Africa. He told me of being there and having been invited to dinner at the home of a Christian convert who had been changed over from being a cannibal to the Christian religion. The home was up on stilts and you climbed up to it on a slatted, leaning, climbing board like chicken houses used to have in them to enable the chickens to climb up at night to roost. He got up there all right and sat with the family. He said when he looked around the stilted enclosure, he saw dried human heads hanging all around the fringes of the place.

I said, "Bishop, what was your reaction?"

His reply was that he sat there and prayed, and that his prayer consisted mainly of one statement: "Oh Lord, while I am here, please don't let this fellow backslide."

ORDERING A STEAK

After he retired and was not traveling so much, I used to get Bishop Arthur Moore to have lunch with me at least once a month. He liked to go to a place called Herren's on Luckie Street in downtown Atlanta. He had gotten a bit shaky and had some real difficulty in cutting his meat, so I suggested to him that he order Salisbury steak. It is largely hamburger and not as difficult to cut. When I suggested it to him, he said, "Son, let me give you some good advice. Never order a steak that has an adjective on it. They are covering up something." I enjoyed these lunches with him for it enabled me to get my spiritual battery recharged. It needed it, too.

DING-DONG BELL

Griffin Bell has been retained as counsel for President Bush in some controversy. Griffin is a Democrat and was Attorney General under President Jimmy Carter. So it was interesting to note that an outgoing Republican President used a Democratic lawyer for his adviser. It is a real tribute to Griffin. He and I have been friends for many years, and for him I had a nickname which was Ding-Dong (taken of course from the nursery rhyme).

While in office he told me that mail in Washington is handled differently from the handling in private circles. Some guy opens your mail and brings it in to you ready to be read. The guy told Griffin one day that like all public officials he got his share of "nut letters" and they never brought those in. He said some nut kept writing him and addressing him as "Ding-Dong" and they were keeping all the "nut letters" including the Ding-Dong ones in a separate file.

Griffin's response was, "Bring me in those Ding-Dong letters."

The letters had simply been my effort to tell him how to run the office up there. What to do and what not to do. That from a guy like me who had never even been in the attorney general's office was indication enough that the letters should be included in the "nut letter" file.

MORE WITH DING-DONG

Ding-Dong and I were playing golf on the famous Burning Tree course near Washington one day when a messenger rode up and said, "Judge Bell, the White House is calling you on the phone." His response was, "The White House is a building. It cannot make telephone calls. If it is some person like Jack Watson, I will talk to him later but if it is President Carter, of course, I will come immediately."

He did not go and kept on playing golf.

THAT GREAT GUY JAKE WARD

Today I had lunch at the Varsity Jr. with my old buddy Judson Clement Ward, affectionately referred to by all who know him as Jake. It was great. He has a good insight on nearly every subject you can think of and it makes me say to myself, "I somehow never thought of that but old Jake is right about it." And he is.

He told me a story about the gate of Heaven where St. Peter stood. First guy came up and said, "I am a Methodist preacher." The Saint said, "Step aside." The second man said, "I am a Baptist preacher," and Pete said, "Step aside." The third guy stepped up and said, "I am a bus driver." St. Peter said, "Come right in and take one of the high seats, for you have scared the hell out of more folks than these other two guys combined."

Yep, Old Jake is a fixture and you just cannot imagine what Emory would be were he not there.

WAY BACK YONDER

In August of 1933 when I began to practice law there was a lawyer not too much older that I named Estes Doremus. He was an associate at one of the larger firms. On the glass door of the entrance to the firm the names of the partners were printed in gold letters. Then there was a black line and below the line were the names of the young associates. There was only one name below the line in this case and it was Estes Doremus. Not knowing the lawyers as we later did we did not know Estes Doremus and we thought the language Estes Doremus was the Latin motto of the firm and meant, "In God We Trust," or, "We Never lose" or, "Never Look Back For Something Might Be Gaining On You." We were relieved when we met Estes Doremus face to face.

AN OBIT EDITOR

Sports editors, columnists and other newspaper celebrities, I am sure, get all kinds of "fan mail" from admirers, but the other day I wrote a fan letter to one who as a newspaper man I bet never has received a fan letter before. The fellow is Tom Bennett, the obituary editor of the Constitution. I told him what a great job he does in keeping me informed as to who among my friends and acquaintances are no longer among us. He gets facts about their lives that I had long forgotten and presents this information concisely and sans flowery language daily. I told him his stuff is the first I turn to each day. He informs me of who the late "him" or "her" was married to, who his or her parents were and what survivors there are among the family members. You forget these things sometimes and it is good to be reminded and brought up to date. I told him I was not anxiously awaiting to become a subject of his writings. More power to you Tom, and may you get other "fan letters."

8

Tips for Living

I broke the little handle on the zipper of my pants. Being fresh out of extra zipper handles I brought into service a gem clip. It served well and at Sunday School one day a lady said to me, "You have dropped a gem clip." I said to her, "Oh, thank you, but I am collecting them."

By the way, let me really recommend the gem clip for such purposes because after all when you have got to get in, you have got to get in.

PASS IT ON

I ran across the following the other day and pass it on:
"If you hear a kind word said of a worthy soul you know,
It may fill his heart with sunshine if you simply tell him so."

That to me is not bad advice for we seem to take greater joy in telling others bad things we hear and omit the telling of the good. I am gonna try it.

LABOR SAVING SUGGESTION

When getting on an elevator let all the others on it at the same time punch their floors first for someone may punch yours and save you that burdensome chore.

TELEPHONE CALLERS

Maybe you too have been plagued as have I in recent months with phone calls at night and at all odd hours from someone who wants me to invest in this or that. They start out calling me by my first name when I have no idea who they are or what they want. To get rid of them just start speaking a bit more loudly and say, "Hello, hello, hello," as if you can't hear them and then hang up. They want to sell securities, get you to join this or that, or to make some gift to the charity they represent. I believe in giving liberally to charities but I make my own selection and not through unknown telephone callers.

DON'T SPILL THE COFFEE

Some of us as we get older get sort of shaky. If you carry a cup of coffee from the kitchen or breakfast room to another room in which to drink it as you read the paper in the morning, I find holding it in my right hand is steadier than in my left. Don't carry the saucer, but instead carry a small bowl in which to place the cup. Some will drip regardless and it is better to drip into a small bowl than a saucer. Try it and see what I am talking about.

PRUNE JUICE CARE

I like prune juice and drink some every day usually at breakfast. Let me warn you not to shake it up. I did the other day and let me tell you it foamed and fizzed like you have never seen. Got all over me, the table, the mat, the floor, and anything else in range. Drink it but by no means ever shake the bottle unless you want trouble on your hands.

COLD HANDS

Lately my hands are always cold. Why, I don't know, but it is true. I have found several ways to warm them but these ways are not always readily available. For instance, the heater in my car is good if you turn it up high and put your hands right close to the vent. At night I can let them rest on my manly hairless chest but again, I am not always in bed. Then there are other hand warming sources such as my open fire at home and some others that are by no means continually available but very acceptable. Has this happened to you? How do you warm them? And along this line I yet agree with the old expression, I don't mind the weather if the wind don't blow.

SLEEP HABITS AND CUSTOMS

Took me a long time to learn it but I now know that it is really great if at night you raise the window in your bedroom so the fresh air comes in. Turn off any heat in the room and get under plenty of cover. It will go a long way towards helping a guy sleep better. Then, there is another sleep comfort, and that is to keep by your bedside a pair of heavy woolen socks and wear them at night while in bed. I guess everybody likes to be sort of cuddly cozy when in the hay and believe me that goes a long way toward getting you there.

Do you have a better sleeping side? I have found that sleeping on my right side is more comfortable to me than on the left, and also that I hear better out of my right ear than my left — so if you sleep on your right side, with the right ear to the pillow you also cut out a lot of noise that might otherwise tend to disturb your sleep. If I don't sleep immediately at night but just lie there, I think it bad for me to get up and read or do something else so as to encourage sleep. Instead it awakens me even more and I go through the whole process again. I like a pendulum tick-tocking clock in my bedroom too. That steady rhythm will frequently induce sleep where nothing else will, but be sure and don't wind the part that sounds the hour during the night. It will disturb you. If it strikes an hour earlier than you think it should be you say, "Man, I have got to get on back to sleep" and you fight it but if it strikes later than you thought it was you say, "Well, it isn't any use to try to get back to sleep now — it is too close to time to get up." You are a loser either way.

TEARS

Some folks seem to be brought to tears more easily than some others. I guess I come in the easy to cry group. I remember my mother was that way. She would talk to me even after I was grown about something and I would say, "Well, Mama you ought not to cry about it." They were not really tears of abject sorrow but tears sometimes of joy and yet other times tears brought on by memories of things past which had a deep significance and were now gone. Certain songs made my wife Ellen and me cry. For instance, a singing of "Silent Night" at Christmas would not infrequently bring tears to my eyes and I would realize that they were in Ellen's as well. The singing of "How Great Thou Art" seems always now to bring tears to my eyes since Ellen loved it so much and they sang it at her funeral. Vivid memories of lost loved ones, situations relived and other things cause me easily to cry. Yet others I know and even members of my own family don't seem to cry as easily. I do not recall my daddy crying. I really don't regret crying. I am actually sort of glad I am that way. To me it makes memories more vivid and meaningful. I fuss at myself and say, "Well, Henry, you don't have to cry about it." But then on the other hand I reckon I am actually glad that I do. To lead a dry-eyed life would not be nearly as good as to lead a teary one.

STORY TELLERS

Just as in most other things some folks can tell a story and make it real interesting and others can tell the same story and bore you to pieces with the telling. In the first place beware of a fellow who starts off by saying, "Let me tell you a real funny story." If you want to tell a story, tell it. If it is funny the hearers will laugh and enjoy it. Saying in advance it is a funny story takes away from the interest and effectiveness of the story. Another thing is to try and get it over with. Don't string it out to the point where everyone is bored with the details before the meat in the coconut is revealed. Another thing to me is don't flub up the punch line. A person would have learned pretty early on whether he can or cannot tell stories. If he cannot do so, let someone who can do so tell them. Bob Hope, Milton Berle and others were great comedians but for instance, if I tried to say those same things it would fall flatter than a flounder. Some can tell them and some can't. Try early to learn which you are.

GO WITH THE GRAIN

I have found that if you want to tear an article out of your newspaper you can tear pretty straight if you tear from the top of the page toward the bottom; but, if you tear it from right to left or vice-versa, you will run into trouble and mess up the piece you are trying to tear out nearly every time.

ANOTHER TIME SAVER

If you are for instance tearing off the top of a package of artificial sugar or the like, don't tear the top all the way off. Do it almost all the way and you have but one piece of trash to dispose of. If you are a regular user of such products, this approach should save you about ten minutes a year.

OPEN WOOD FIRES AT HOME

They are definitely on the wane but let me tell you I do love an open wood fire at home. In fact, I like them so much that I have one nearly every night during the fall and winter months. I like to sit in front of the open fire, watch the flames flicker in ever changing patterns and just muse a bit. It is even better if you turn out all the lights in the room and the fire furnishes all of the illumination. Man that is great. You can just sit there and meditate, think (if you are capable of such), ponder, go back over old times and even plan ahead (but not too much planning ahead — fires are conducive to thinking of past and not the future). You put a couple of sticks of pine on the bottom when you lay the fire and a couple of oak sticks on the top. Pine burns fast, catches the oak and it burns slowly. As it dies down you throw on another log and there is a prompt flare up of fire.

The flame patterns change continually as the fire gets further and further along and really there is nothing as I see it just like it. Now a lot of my friends either because they are lazy or extravagant or ornery have installed what they refer to as "gas logs" a contraption consisting of some artificial logs (they don't really look too much like a log) which burn natural gas when lighted. To me it is artificial, expensive, and not the genuine article. There is no change in the flame flickering pattern and you cannot toss on another log. You are stuck with what you see and that is what you get. Selah.

GETTING UPSET OVER THINGS

It took me a long time to get there but I did. I no longer worry and fret and get upset over anything. I mean anything. If I get in a traffic jam and have a long wait I say to myself, "Bowden, you have got to sit somewhere so why not here?" I can do nothing about it. Fretting simply upsets me further and so I just relax and wait patiently. If I start to the farm and forget my keys I just go back and get them. I don't chide myself or get all frothy about it but just take it as a part of a normal day. I am telling you it is a great decision to reach in your life and I urge it on you. Let nothing upset you. It is great for your heart and now that I have been told I have one, I plan to care better for it.

ONE STEP AT A TIME

One definition of perspective I guess is "the point from which something is observed." The closer you are the more detail you see. The further away the broader picture you see. Thus one's impression of anything seen is closely associated with the point from which the object is observed. For instance, the folks who live in Charing, Georgia, are scared when they go to the big town of Macon while the folks in Macon are a bit scared when they go to the big town of Atlanta and similarly, the folks in Atlanta are scared contemplating a trip to the even larger town of New York. It depends on where you are coming from. Looking out of my office window I can see some 15 miles away; Stone Mountain is on the distant horizon. It gives the appearance of a small mound. But when you are at its base it becomes the huge monolith that it is, awesome in its full dimensions. When you look at the ground from an airplane, it all looks flat but when you get down there you find hills, valleys, meadows and all sorts of impediments.

In order to try to make things which I call monumental tasks a bit easier for me, I try to break them down into one-step-at-a-time units, and to behold the next step is not nearly as likely to overwhelm me as is the tendency to look at the whole big task at one time.

QUICK OIL CHANGE

Took my pickup truck to one of these Jiffy Lube places this a.m. before coming to the office. Turned out to be really good. Got the oil changed, the truck greased, the filter changed, another gimmick replaced that keeps water from getting into the oil and the tires were checked for pressure and the like. It all cost less than 40 bucks and took only about 20 minutes. The truck runs better, sounds better and I believe is better. I recommend the use of such places.

THIS BUSINESS OF AGE

I have known some folks who were, insofar as age goes, 80 when they were 50, and yet others who were 50 when they were 80. My formula has always been to keep always something to do. Outline on notes what you would like to get done and set about the job of doing those things. Oh, I know that sometimes you don't feel like doing these things but I say force yourself to do it and soon you get a feeling of accomplishment that in itself serves to stimulate you. Never say, "Oh, I can't do that, I am too old." Keep on at it until you have proven by trying that you cannot do it. Oh, I know that orthopedic and other physically disabling ailments can prevent you from doing certain things but if such is true, blame it not on old age but on the ailment. Another thing, be upbeat about life in general. Never grouse or complain or grouch about something if it can possibly be avoided.

Yesterday afternoon (for instance) my list included painting two small footstools, cleaning out the trunk of my car, straightening out the interior of the garage and boxing and stacking the kindling in my wood supply getting ready for the fall and winter season ahead. It was Sunday and I got them all done and then went to a friend's for dinner getting home and to bed by ten. And I felt much better for having a sensation of accomplishment. I believe it is excellent therapy. I want to wear out and not rust out. Selah.

PATTING

There is a significant difference between "patting" and "petting." Maybe you never thought about it like that. One pets an animal such as a dog or cat or whatever animal you choose to pet. But patting usually takes place between two adults. Of course I know also that one "pets" an infant. But patting is a different sort of thing. When you see a wife reach over and pat her husband it makes you have a feeling that is good and approving and makes you feel a warmth toward the couple that is definitely there. The same applies of course when the husband pats the wife. Or it may be that it is a parent patting an older child. Patting enables the person doing the patting to express tangibly a feeling of approval and affection. It causes the person patted to be again reassured of the approval and affection by the one doing the patting. It is sad to realize but when you lose your spouse you miss this patting process far beyond what you had ever imagined. You no longer have someone whom it is your God-given right and really God-given obligation to pat. To pat other adults than your spouse often causes raised eyebrows so you don't do it. So, if you still have free and full patting rights and privileges with another don't fail to exercise them and do it often.

SUGGESTIONS TO CHILDREN
(AND ADULTS TOO, I GUESS)

It is too much to ask of a child, who is to say the least immature, that the child do certain things in order better to relate to others, and especially to adults, but there are some simple things which would go a long way toward making children well liked. Everyone wishes to be well thought of by others. These are some of those things which occur to me:

(a) When you see another person look that person straight in the face and do not look down at the floor or off into the wild blue yonder;

(b) Call the person clearly by name since everyone likes to be identified by his or her name;

(c) Say, "Yes ma'am" or, "Yes sir" if the person is an adult;

(d) Always say at the appropriate place, "Thank You" or, "Please" or, "No, thank you."

(e) Where a lady is present always let her precede you through a door after opening it first for her; and

(f) When being seated it is in order always to pull out the chair and assist the lady in being seated before seating yourself. There are of course other niceties which could be added but this is enough as a starter and I am sure such would enable a child (or an adult) to gain favor with others much more quickly.

EXPRESS YOUR FEELINGS IF GOOD

There are so many folks for whom I have a sincere feeling of affection or admiration. I have noticed that whenever someone expresses love or affection or appreciation to me it boosts my spirits and sort of makes my day. That makes me feel that I myself am terribly guilty of not expressing my good feeling toward others more frequently than I do. If you love somebody, say so. Husband and wife take each other too much for granted. The attitude is, "Sure I love you, I married you didn't I?" But that is not the way to do it. Keep on saying I love you. We all like to hear it. If people have done a fine job, tell them so. If their attire compliments them, tell them so. If they are good car drivers, tell them they are. What a difference it makes.

On the other hand, if you disapprove or if you see some mistakes made, remain silent unless they ask for comment. Your silence may speak even more eloquently than your words. This is hard to do. The tendency is to say, "Hey, you knuckle-head, what in the world made you do that?" Don't say it.

GETTING THE BLUES

Don't worry if you sometimes get what we call "The Blues" and feel sort of at odds with life itself. Forget it. That is natural. That is the way nature is. We have high mountains and we have low valleys, we have tides that come in and also go out. We have rain and we also have sunshine. We have winter and we also have summer. That is the way the world is organized and it will always be that way. The best way to get over the blues as I see it is to first check up on your physical situation. Eating enough? Eating too much? Getting too much exercise or not enough? Next, get your attitude changed. Sulking? Get happy. Just decide you will be happy and do it. Quit griping and emphasize the good things in your life. Start counting the things for which you can truly be thankful. Your home, wife, husband, job, children, friends, and opportunities and begin to count your blessings. As the hymn says, "Count your many blessings, name them one by one, and it will surprise you what the Lord has done." Do these things and others too and you will soon find that you are over the blues. Oh, they will come back just as night will follow day but there is something you can do about it. If you are a lady go out and buy yourself a pretty new frock.

VITAMINS

Don't know why the doctors are seemingly reluctant to prescribe vitamins for their patients. I bought me some of different kinds and have been taking them now daily for some months and to me it seems they provide me with more energy than I had prior to taking them. Not knowing whether they would hurt you I called a doctor friend of mine and asked him. He said, "No, they won't hurt you," and indicated that if I felt they were helping me to go on and take them. So that is what I am doing. I seem to remember that when Bing Crosby was in his very prime he had some song in which a part of one of the lines went like this, "For I'm full of Vitamin A, Oh." I plan to continue the procedure for at my age I will take any steps to stimulate the spring in my step and add an ounce to my bounce.

LISTENING TO THE BIBLE

I am for the third or fourth time listening to the reading of the Bible on tape. It is an amazing thing. I am now in Exodus. Every time I reread it there is something brought home to me that I sort of brushed over in earlier listenings. In Genesis and Exodus for instance, there is deceit, absurdity, telling of lies, incest, and other evils and I have come across folks going back on their word and lots of other things. You can get the Bible on tape from the Episcopal Radio and TV Center in Atlanta from the Rev. Mr. Scheudigg and I recommend it. Forget what it costs. It is read by Alexander Scourbev and he is superb. There are lots of Bible expressions I like and wish were used today more frequently, such as lo and behold, and it came to pass, sojourn, beget, and bring forth. The men it seems beget and the women are the ones who bring forth. I am glad it is so arranged. Begetting is one thing but Bringing Forth is quite another. Everybody to his own calling.

9

Farm Stuff

If you have never lived on a farm or visited one at length you may not know what is coming in this report. Farmers, when asked what time they work, say frequently, "From can to can't." That means they start early in the a.m. when you can first see and you work all day until the sun goes down and you can't see. That is a pretty long day but it applies usually to the growing season and not to the long winter months. There were three meals on the farm which were breakfast, dinner and supper. They never called the noon time meal lunch or such fancy name but it was dinner. They were working in the fields and when the noonday hour arrived and it was time to eat, the farmer's wife went out on the back porch of the farmhouse and pulled a rope which brought into action the "farm bell," which the men working in the field could hear and it meant, "Dinner is ready — come on in." They came too, hungry as bears. Then after dinner they were back at the fields doing what they were doing. Then about sundown they came on back to the house and had supper which, of course, included cornbread, "sawmill" gravy, meat, and peach or apple pie for the dessert.

The size of a farm was expressed not so much in acres as the number of "hands" it took to operate it. All farm employees were referred to as hands and the farm would be as far as size is concerned referred to as a "two-hand" farm.

On a farm you "chopped" cotton and "plowed" corn. Chopping meant going down the cotton row and chopping out grass and weeds so they would not sap the food and fertilizer meant for the cotton. For corn you plowed between the rows of growing corn to accomplish the same results.

The farmer would tell his wife where he would be working that day such as "down on the lower forty" or "up on the high ground." The number forty referred to the acres in a known area on the farm.

Then there is a term common and well-known to farmers but which most city folks are completely unfamiliar. It is "lay by." One may ask another, "When are you gonna lay by?" The term means that you have planted, fertilized, chopped the cotton, plowed the corn, and done all else in the cultivation process and you were gonna quit further work of that sort and await nature to produce the crop. The farmer to whom the question was asked may say, "Well, I laid by last week."

On a farm cotton is not graded by how many bolls are on a stalk but by the length of the cotton staple or fiber. A grader pulls a sample from a bale and holding one end between thumb and forefinger of one hand and one at the same place on the other hand he keeps pulling the fibers back and forth until he gets them all parallel and the length of the fiber determines the grade of the cotton. Such grades as "fair" or "middling" or "fancy" or "long" are used. That is how when you ask somebody how he feels and he may say "fair to middling" got started. You ain't sick and yet you don't feel on top.

So you can see that farming is a tough life but the true farmer loves it. Like a lot of other things, for instance, being a doctor, it is rewarding to the practitioner I know but it would not be my cup of tea. There are lots of folks who feel the same way about being a lawyer, but it appealed to me from the start and I have enjoyed my so called career as one. Others would detest it. That is what makes the world go round.

⟝⟞

ABOUT PLOWING

I don't know whether you have ever lived in the country, but if you have then this is old stuff to you. If not, it will be new. There are some plows which are called two-horse plows, but not many. Mainly the plows are called one-horse plows but strangely it is seldom you can get a horse to do plowing with the same earnestness that a mule will give to it. It should really be called a "one-mule plow." A plow is usually a wooden instrument with two long handles side by side coming down to a point at the ground. They are usually made of wood and where the plow "stock" hits the ground is a place where one of several different types of plow "shares" are attached to the stock. The plow has what is called a single tree attached to it and from the mule's collar traces of either chain or leather come straight back and hook to the single tree. When the mule walks forward the farmer jabs the point of the plow share into the ground and as the mule progresses the plow share does its work of digging into the soil. It can be a mold board plow share designed to really go deep and turn over the soil or it can be a turn share which will only turn over a shallower cut or it can be a row share which will dig a trench into which seed will later be placed to be the basis of the crop.

Now let me say that a horse is not nearly as suited to plowing as a mule. The mule is heavy, strong, placid usually and will keep on pulling as long as the farmer is back there at the plow. At the end of a row the farmer will say either gee, meaning turn right, or haw, meaning turn left. And if you don't think a mule knows these commands you just ain't been there. Mules didn't have fancy names like race horses. Mules were usually named something like Claude, Smokey, White Eye, Maude, Ginger, Big Foot, or Garrett.

The plow, mule and farmer are all turned around and go back the way they came to plow another furrow parallel with the last one and this keeps on until the whole field is plowed. The reason horses are not as good as mules for plowing is that a horse is a lot more frisky, gets tired more easily, spooks pretty easily (by spooking I mean jumping at some movement or sound that is unfamiliar) and when a horse thinks he has plowed enough, he just stops and won't plow any more and that is called a balk. A horse will sho do it. A mule is the progeny of a horse for a mother and a jackass for a father. (I heard some disgruntled lady say all fathers are jackasses. I have no comment on that.) Now I am also told that if the father is a horse and the mother is a lady jackass — maybe a jackassette — then the offspring is not a mule but a jenny. You had better check me on that one — doesn't sound too close to accurate. When you bring in a mule from a day of plowing and turn him loose, free of harness and all — he will usually lie down on the ground, stick his four legs up in the air and roll back and forth in the dust. He is tired and has got to get his night's rest to be ready the next day to respond properly to the gees and the haws.

SECOND CHAPTER ON PLOWING

Maybe you have heard the expression, "I am as tired as if I had spent the whole day plowing new ground." Farms don't just come ready for plowing. The fields in their primitive stages were either woods which have been clean cut and cleared or were rocky barren spaces full of weeds and briars. The cutting and raking, clearing of the trees, underbrush and such from ground never having been subjected to a plow of any kind is referred to as "plowing new ground" because it is new to plow cultivation. And when you make the first run over the land with a big turning plow, the plow hits rocks, roots, gravel and all sorts of things, sometimes even breaking the plow stock or plow share. It is tough on the mule and the plowman and tends to make a farmer who is given over to such to begin cussing. A day of plowing new ground and both a farmer and his mule are plum "wo out" and each needs his night of rest before going back at it the next morning soon after sun up. If you have read this far you have read all your groveling scrivener knows about plowing and you can tell that is not much.

HOG KILLING

If you have never been to a hog killing and are not squeamish, go to one. I went to one as a lad while in the country. They kill hogs in cold weather usually. In this one they just walked up to the hog, cut his throat with a sharp knife, waited till he fell over dead and plunged him into a vat of really hot water and began to do all that is then required to dismember a hog. I said "him," but it may have been a lady hog as far as I know. Makes no difference to a real tough hog killer, you know.

They use or sell everything about the hog but the squeal. I don't feel that I want to attend another, but am glad I at least have seen one and know how it is done and can now make my own decision to stay away.

BILLY THE GOAT

I don't see any goats these days. When I was a lad I had a goat. Guess what his name was — that's right, "Billy." And I had a small wagon to which I hitched him and pulled the wagon to my delight and that of all the other little squirts in the neighborhood. Wonder what ever happened to old William.

MILK FROM GOATS

I've got a friend by the name of Roe Nall. He is the pastor of a black Methodist church in Lithonia, Georgia. He has two daughters, each of whom is allergic to milk. So he has to provide for them goat's milk. I lent him my truck for the purpose of enabling him to haul his mama goats up to north Georgia to visit their husbands. I told him that I only knew of two breeds of goats, one the Toggenberg and the other the Alpine. What were his? He told me what he used mainly were Alpine but that he has a couple of Toggenbergs also in reserve. I told him I reckon the milking of those goats is not easy because their teats are so small. He said yes, they are about the size of your little finger — but he gets about a gallon a day each. That seems to me like a whole lot of goat milk coming from one Toggenberg. There are a lot of strange goings on in this world and that's one of them.

A NEW EXPERIENCE

Last week I had a new experience. I put milk on my cereal as I do each morning but for the first time in my life the milk that I used was goats' milk brought to me by Roe Nall. I still don't see how you can get enough of a grip on a goat's teat to produce a flow of milk, but then I am sort of cow-oriented instead of being goaty.

I could not distinguish any difference in goats' milk and cows' milk. Goats milk is sold in the grocery stores now just like cows' milk.

STOMPING CLODS

We used to get a man with a mule to come and plow up our garden in the spring so as to get it ready for planting. It was always a thrill to me to see that day come. I would walk along behind the plow and with my bare feet I would step on and break up the clods that the plow turned up. The soil was always moist and cool and the clods had not hardened so that it was a lot of fun getting this done. In actuality it helped in the process of soil preparation. I guess today they do it with a motor driven plow which does make a noise but it does not make the same snorting noises the mule made. Also you have to turn it at the end of the row for no motor driven plow that I have ever seen responds to the commands "gee" and "haw."

SIMPLE LANGUAGE

Cows and horses breed, fish are said at certain times of year to be bedding, hogs I am told are in rutting season, while monkeys and humans mate. Seems it would be simpler to eliminate all this varied language and just substitute the language "carrying on." It would be a whole lot simpler.

ROBERT AND ROBERTA

Maybe you did not know some of these things either: The way to tell the difference between a male and female bobwhite is that the male has a white throat and the female a yellow one. Bet you've been worrying about that for weeks.

MORE DIFFERENCES

When I was a lad I observed that when a cow is lying down and wants to arise, it gets up with its hind legs first. Now a horse does just the opposite. If you didn't know that you are uninformed and probably doomed.

MILKING TIME

At about five in the afternoon I would have to come home to milk our cow whose name was Red Eye. Some of my buddies would come along to watch. I always milked on the cow's right side into a quart cup and when it was filled, I would empty it into the big bucket I kept on the shelf so if Red Eye kicked she would only damage at most a quart. While my buddies watched eagerly I would, on occasion turn the cow's teat toward them and squirt milk on them. I could shoot it about ten or twelve feet. They learned to keep their distance.

A good cow was supposed to have a calf about every year. After some months of producing a good supply, the cow would "go dry" as they called it which meant she was no longer giving milk. My daddy would say to me, "Son, after school this afternoon I want you to take old Red Eye out to Col. Zadock Harrison's to be serviced." I didn't know what being serviced meant. I thought they might be gonna trim her tail, polish her hooves (cows have cloven hooves while horses do not), but some years later I learned what he was talking about and was glad I had been a part of the process. I would put a halter on Red Eye, tie a rope to it and start walking the two or three miles out there. I had to pass the houses of some pretty girls along Ponce de Leon and Moreland Avenues, so I always walked on the opposite side of the cow and stooped low so as not to be seen.

A few days later I would go back for her but her tail didn't seem to have been trimmed or her hooves polished. It made no real difference to me, the unenlightened one. In the gestation period we would get a second cow.

When I went out to get old Red Eye after she was serviced she always seemed to be docile and satisfied.

SHE GORED ME GOOD

When I was about five years old, I had a little red coat. It was a little red coat because I was little. They say cows don't like red and the one we had named Blackie must have followed that tradition for she got me down one day in the backyard and was goring me in the head in really good fashion. My grandpa (his name was Anthony Asbury Turner, and since his initials were A.A., I later always referred to him as either Two-A or A Square Turner) saw my plight and was able to rescue me from the crumpled horns of old Blackie. Still have the mark of that goring on my aching empty head.

BLACKIE'S DEMISE

My dad tied Blackie to a limb of a tree (don't ever do that) and she would go round and round as she grazed, and she got finally so tied up she lost her balance and old Blackie hanged herself. We found her dead in the afternoon hanging from the tree.

CHICKENS

In my youth, which was a long time ago, lots of folks, including my daddy, raised chickens in their yards even in the city. We had a fenced-off area in the back known as the chicken yard. Chickens come in lots of breeds. There are white leghorns, barred rock, dominicker, Plymouth Rock, Rhode Island reds (to my father's great disappointment I always referred to them as Red Eyed Rolands). Every chicken grower seems to have his favorite.

My daddy was devoted to black minorcas. They were pretty good sized chickens with black feathers. I believe they also laid eggs more brown than white. We kept in the kitchen a lard bucket into which Mama put all the table scraps. We called it the chicken bucket and Daddy would take it out each morning and feed the contents to his flock. There was a little house in the corner of the chicken yard into which chickens would go to roost at night. They had a pole with 12-inch slats nailed across it leaning up to the "roost." The fowls would climb it, and I don't see how, each night about dusk and roost on another horizontal pole all night until crowing time in the morning.

I never have understood how a chicken would sleep while standing all night with its feet clasped around a pole. Seems like when sleep came they would lose their balance and fall. But God made them that way and they do it, I can assure you. Never ever heard of a chicken falling off a roost.

When enough eggs had accumulated, a "setting hen" would begin sitting on the several eggs in her nest and would stay there until the biddies, as little chickens were called, were hatched out. Little chickens were cute as could be. Today they do it with incubators instead of setting hens. They get more chickens that way but it ain't nearly as much fun. I am glad they have not carried it over into the human of the species, though I have read where they are approaching it.

Chickens provided not only eggs for the family but also meat and my mama would say, "Son, go out and wring the neck of that biggest black minorca hen and bring it on in here so I can get it prepared for our Sunday dinner." So obeying to the letter anything Mama said do, I would go out, corner the hen (or sometimes a rooster) grab it by the neck and swing it round and round till body and head were separated and take the chicken in to Mama. I couldn't possibly do that now, but it was my job in those days and I thought nothing of it.

I had a friend named Jack Jetton who lived a few doors up

the street and he was deathly afraid of a wrung chicken head, so of course, I would always take the head up there to scare him with it. The same applied to turkey heads. Today I am too "chicken hearted" to do any such as that. Families in those days frequently bought live turkeys for Thanksgiving and Christmas feasting and kept them in the chicken yard, fattening them up for the feast day to come and you could hear the turkeys up and down the street gobbling daily, little realizing that they were nearing the end of their red-necked lives.

Talking about eggs, have you ever noticed in one of these short-order breakfast places like a Huddle House, Waffle House and such that when you order eggs the cook often picks up an egg and with one hand breaks it and plops it on to the grill. That must take a lot of practice. If I tried it, egg would be all over me and most of the customers. But they do it routinely.

MORE ON CHICKENS AND ODD TRIVIA

Human eyelids come down from the top — so when you close your eyes you lower your eyelids. Unless I am badly mistaken or have forgotten my youthful observations a chicken's eyelids come up from below and are just the reverse of ours. Thus, where we lower our eyelids, chickens raise theirs. Also, the eggs you buy at the supermarket will not hatch in an incubator or under a setting hen because they are laid in hen yards where the hens are not rooster-exposed.

BUTTERMILK

My mama created the very best buttermilk I ever tasted. We had a good sized crockery churn and all the excess milk was placed in it and when it "turned" it was ready for churning. My mama could tell you when it had "turned" but I couldn't. The top of the churn had a wooden cover (round with a hole in the middle). The dasher was a stick like a broomstick with a wooden cross piece at the bottom. You would put the end of the dasher through the hole in the wooden top to the churn and the cross piece down inside.

Then it was my task to get busy churning. This was done by plunging the dasher down and up into the turned milk. The noise it made was about like this: "Casloonk, casloonk, casloonk." You kept at it until the butter in the milk rose to the top and Mama would remove it and put in a dish to add a bit of salt and the like. You kept on churning until all the butter but a few flecks had been removed and you had the very best buttermilk I ever tasted. We had our own milk, our own butter, and our own buttermilk all the time when I was growing up. Churning was not always convenient in that I would rather have been playing ball but Mama said churn and I got busy churning.

BEAVERS

On my farm in Meriwether County near Greenville, Georgia, my man told me that someone had built a pond. I already had one of about an acre and a half and had authorized no one to build further. He said this pond was built of all things by the beavers. I went to look at it and you wouldn't believe what I saw. The varmints had cut down trees, felled them in a straight line, filled in the openings with mud and debris and had built a dam across the small creek that is now at least some 20 acres in size. Thought about dynamiting it but if I did so it would throw all that water on the lower riparian owners and might cause damage to crops or pastures in which event they might sue me. I then had my man make several holes in the dam to let water out gradually. The eager beavers had it repaired the next morning. The bases of my trees are under water to a depth of a foot or two and the foresters say that will kill the trees unless I can get something done to remove the water. I have now been in touch with some beaver trappers. They have a system that they know and they can either kill the beavers or remove them to another area. I wish the trappers well but as many times as I have been there I have never seen a single beaver. They must be under water, hiding in the woods or off gallivanting with some other beavers. I am anxious to know what is going to happen to my beavers and their pond.

SPLIT RAIL FENCES

Easily built, long-lasting and generally picturesque, split rail fences are pretty common throughout the countryside. They are usually three to four rails high, run in zigzag courses and the ends overlap as much or as little as is desired. But countrymen will tell you that not all rails are suitable for such fences. For instance, pine won't do. It deteriorates too fast. But locust, oak, cedar, and ash make good rails. Locust, they say, lasts the longest but it is not as easy to find in sufficient quantities. Lots of folks drive metal 3- or 4-foot spikes where the rails come together to hold them in place and I have found that to be a good approach. This is not a requirement but it does help to keep the rails from blowing off or being knocked off by cattle. You don't have to paint them, you can replace one rail at a time as needed. The more weathered they get the more attractive they are. It is a good deal and I recommend it.

HOW DO CHICKENS CHEW?

When I was a lad I asked my daddy what kind of teeth a chicken has. And he told me they don't have any teeth. I asked him how do they chew their food. He said that chickens have what we call a craw. Now a craw is a little sack down in the gizzard and all the food the chicken eats passes through the craw which the chicken has filled up with sand and grit to masticate the food.

Say, that is the origin of the old expression, "Man, what's sticking in your craw." When something goes wrong and we're hard to get along with, we've gotten accustomed to saying, "Man, what's sticking in your craw?"

10

On the Road

A longtime friend and client of mine, Mrs. Olga Six Baker, lived in Baxley (Appling County), Georgia, on US #1, north of town where she owned and operated a place called Bay Creek Farms. Her husband had been dead for a number of years. They had no children. She was a fine lady. Like a lot of other ladies, for some unknown reason she did not like to have anyone know her age. She died on August 10, 1991, and the funeral was scheduled for August 15 at 11 a.m.

I drove Irene, my 1989 Ford pickup truck, which is a great vehicle, from Atlanta to be there on Wednesday the 14th of August. I went down I-75 and since it led through Forsyth, Georgia (Monroe County), which was the home of my parents, I decided to stop off for a moment or two and see what the old town looked like. Lots of changes have taken place there since they were married in the First Methodist Church on February 25, 1903. My dad's father was pastor of that church. I drove all through the town. The courthouse where I assume my father was admitted to the bar is there. There are lots of modern and pretty homes there now and I wondered which of those homes were there when they lived there. I also wondered how my mama and daddy met. I am sure he was stricken with her for she was a beautiful girl. I have pictures of her taken at that time. Folks were so formal in those days. She called him Mr. Wightman and he called her Miss Mattie Leigh.

Their first child, Mary Bowden, was born on November 3, 1905, and I came along five years later on July 23, 1910. Then my brother, Turner Wightman Bowden, who died at age 6, was born in 1914.

It only takes about a little over an hour to get to Macon. At that point, I got on I-16, which is sparsely traveled and which leads from Macon to Savannah. I always get off at Exit 17 because that is where the famous Sweat's Barbecue is located. I did so this time and enjoyed it. I got to talk to Mr. Sweat, whose daughter Cincy is a nurse at Emory Hospital, and who was one of my nurses some while back on one of my many surgical visits there. She is now married and has a daughter. I bought a bottle of Sweat's great barbecue sauce while there. After my barbecue lunch, I drove on down Highway 19 through Soperton and Vidalia as well as Higgston. I stopped in Soperton at the Dairy Queen and got an ice cream cone. Honestly, they make the best ice cream in the world. It is so creamy and tasty that I said to myself that this is far too good for just old ordinary men such as I to be allowed to eat. It should be reserved for royalty and pretty girls only. Dipped in chocolate it is even better.

When I got to Mrs. Baker's farm I went in and met with Gertrude Desha and Jasper (Red) Dubberly, two of the main beneficiaries under her will, and went over the will with them in detail. I then figured I had better go by the courthouse, meet the judge and get it all set up for the probate after the funeral the next day. I did what I call a dry-run as I like to get it all arranged in advance if possible. It was a good thing I did for the judge's clerk, Mrs. Deal, said the judge, a lady named Mrs. Brock, would not be in that day or the next. She was moving. I got her to call and get the judge to come in on Thursday at noon and meet us all there. That is what she did and the judge very graciously met us at the designated time. I had checked into the Pine Lodge Motel (formerly owned by my client and her husband) and had a nice single room for $29. Then I drove down to Captain Joe's Seafood Restaurant where I had previously dined on another visit. It was an excellent place and I can recommend it heartily. Food and service were good. After supper I called Mary Lamar and got her to have Henry Jr. call me so we could talk over some law stuff, which he did.

At the check out counter at the motel the next morning the man said the best place for breakfast was the Huddle House. It was great. Then to Shell for gas. Maybe you recall that the first self-serve grocery stores were Piggly Wiggly, were begun by a man named Clarence Saunders of Memphis. All of them are self-serve now. Piggly Wiggly has gone out of Atlanta, but believe me they are all over south Georgia. I asked the lady at the filling station how to get to the local Piggly Wiggly. She said to go to the red light, turn left and I would find it right across from Kentucky Fried Chicken. I did just that. Got my bit of shopping done and went out to dry-run on location of the cemetery where the graveside services were scheduled for 11 a.m. I found it. I was the first one there after the undertaker. The tent was up. Got a good parking place and in a short while the other mourners began arriving. Undertaker was man named Bass. He said that the white undertaking establishments handled only white persons and there were two black undertakers for blacks. This is one place where apparently they have not yet integrated. I think the same thing holds true in Atlanta but I don't really know.

There were some 50 people at the funeral. On the front row were Gertrude Desha, the longtime servant and friend of Mrs. Baker, her daughter, and also Jasper Leroy Dubberly, Mrs. Baker's longtime farmer. Rev. James Reese, a friend of Mrs. Baker who now lives at Richmond Hill near Savannah, preached the funeral and did a fine job. At one juncture he stepped aside and a lady came to the front and sang the Lord's Prayer beautifully, without any accompaniment. It turned out that she was one of Jasper

Dubberly's five daughters. It was a sweet service all the way and exactly as I feel Mrs. Baker would have wanted it to be.

After the service was over I went to probate court and met with the judge and her clerk, the two witnesses, Mrs. Elizabeth Diehl from Trust Company in Savannah (the executor), Mr. Guldens, who was Mrs. Baker's CPA, and Mrs. Carolyn Williamson, a longtime friend of Mrs. Baker, who had handled her affairs under a power of attorney while Mrs. Baker had been ill. We got it all done quickly, since I had prepared all of the necessary documents in advance, and we departed. We went back to Mrs. Baker's home where the ladies had prepared a wonderful lunch of baked chicken, fried chicken, ham, black-eyed peas, and all sorts of dessert and iced tea and the like. All of the friends and neighbors sat around the house and talked and discussed Mrs. Baker and how she would have enjoyed being there and seeing them all. It made me realize how good and how neighborly and supportive the people are in small-town America. In contrast I would not recognize my own neighbors if they walked in the door right now for we just don't get to know them in cities like they do in smaller communities. Their way is far better than ours and I think that even though death was involved, I felt really good about all that went on in south Georgia that day.

I mentioned that Mrs. Baker did not like to tell her age. One day a lady asked her how old she was and Mrs. Baker leaned forward, looked both ways, and whispered, "Can you keep a secret?" The lady replied she sure could. Then Mrs. Baker responded, "Well, so can I." That is as close as the inquirer got to finding out Mrs. Baker's age. She was actually 92 when she died.

Another thing about these smaller towns is that everything is central. Mrs. Baker's home and farm are on US #1. So are the cemetery, courthouse, the Pine Lodge Motel, the Shell filling station and the Huddle House where I had breakfast. US #1 in Baxley is just like Peachtree Street in Atlanta.

After leaving Baxley I drove on to Savannah to meet with Mrs. Elizabeth Diehl, who is the trust officer handling the estate, since the Trust Company is the executor.

Upon arriving in Savannah, I checked into the Days Inn on Bay Street so when I finished at the bank I called my cousin Ralph Bowden and his wife Mardi and agreed that we would that night go out to Tybee Island where her wonderfully fine daughter Margaret and her husband Johnny Wylly live. It is about 22 miles out from Savannah. They were terrific hosts and I wish all of my family had been along with me.

Had an unusual experience with Irene, the pickup. I was parked on the side of the expressway reading a map with the door on the driver's side open a bit for light. A big 18-wheeler truck came roaring by and the wind it created blew against the open door, carried it forward and sprung it so it would open only about ten inches. Thus, from then on I had to squeeze my too ample body in through the 10 inch aperture to get in, and reverse it to get out. Not too easy. I am taking it tomorrow to get fixed. Another thing I did I have never done before was to lock my keys up in the truck and I had to get the lock and key man to come and open it for me. He had no trouble and I was off again. Got back from Tybee, visited a while with my cousin Ralph and then to the motel where I read till about 11:30.

Then Tuesday a.m. I was up, out of the motel and on the road by 8 a.m. Drove on to Metter, Georgia, for breakfast. Somehow I had also mistakenly punched the 4-wheel drive button which I had to get the Ford man in Metter to straighten out for me. I had never used the 4-wheel drive on Irene.

I stopped in Dublin to look up my friend Bo Whaley but could not reach him so I drove on home getting to Atlanta by 1:20 from Savannah. While in Lyons, Georgia, I bought some pumpkins, yams, tomatoes and a stalk of sugar cane. My grandkids have never probably seen sugar cane so I will try to educate them a bit. I will also cut out pumpkins for their Halloween celebration. Love to ride through the country and this trip was wonderfully enjoyable. Checked in with Mary Lamar and Henry and Jeanne to let them know the wanderer was home. 'Twas a great trip.

LESSON IN A T-MODEL

You had to crank T-Model Ford cars. They had no batteries for cranking and the whole thing ran on what was called a magneto. It was the monitor of all electricity and everything electrically drew on that magneto. So many people in their moments of bragging toot their own horns to such an extent that it became just plain out depressing. I learned from the old Model T that when you blew the horn in the Ford it dimmed the lights. There is some sort of lesson there it seems to me.

BURMA SHAVE

Looking back, I can remember when Burma Shave came on the market. I never used any but as I rode along in my car from one town to the next, I saw their unique ads with advice and suggestions painted on a crosspiece and nailed to a stick which was driven in the ground. Those that I can remember went something like this:

From New York town to Pumpkin Holler,
Half a pound for half a dollar.

College boys your courage muster,
Shave off that fuzzy cookie duster.

Within this vale of toil and sin,
The head grows bald but not the chin.

TRAVEL TIP

I take along several cassettes of tapes holding ten tapes each and I play them almost constantly as I ride along. They are really great as I see it and I recommend it. Take with you on auto trips two small bags and two of your carryall canvas bags. Put dirty clothes in the canvas bags and daily usable stuff in the two smaller bags.

ORANGE CONES

I have decided that if I were a business school graduate just coming out with my MBA degree the business I would start up would be the manufacturing of orange cones. They are magic and seemingly in short supply for the average citizen. Ride along the street most anywhere and all of a sudden the lane is closed and marked off by strategically placed orange cones. You used to connect them with some street repairs but no longer. Private delivery wagons, automobiles, pickups and maybe even golf carts use them. Why not just keep about four in the trunk of your car and when parking places are in short supply just stop in the middle of the street or anywhere and put your flasher on and place carefully the four cones and you are protected for life. Apparently there is no law against such so why not try it until some meddling legislator says *NO, NO*. Don't knock it. It is a magnificent idea. A telephone truck was in my drive and had cones out. I asked why and he said that the company requires it so he will have to go around the back of the truck to pick up cones when departing and will be able to observe any little children whom he might otherwise back over.

BUBBA DOO

Spur sells gas at less cost than others. I dropped in a Spur station in Lewis Grizzard's hometown of Moreland the other day. It must be sort of an event for someone to buy gas. The station's name was Bubba Doo's Spur Stop. Bubba called out to someone inside and said, "Hey, Flathead, turn on the electricity. Some guy wants some gas pumped." Now if Bubba Doo isn't a redneck name, I have never heard one. He was a sprightly little guy but pleasant with it all and if you ever go through there stop and talk to Bubba and Flathead.

LITTLE WHITE HOUSES

Last Saturday I took my daughter Anne with me and drove to Warm Springs, Georgia, where we visited the Little White House of Franklin Delano Roosevelt when he was president. It was an interesting visit and I recommend it. He was a controversial president to say the least. It seems folks either worshipped him or despised him. I knew both kinds. As far as my preference is concerned he was "our president" and I was for him. He certainly knew more about what was happening than did I. The State of Georgia has done a good job in building a museum there with many artifacts connected with his service and particularly of his stay in Georgia where he found the Warm Springs beneficial to him in his suffering from polio.

I got to thinking about whether there were other "little white houses." I believe President Harry Truman had one in Key West, Florida, and I have visited it also. I do not seem to recall any others. I am not talking about regular homes but special places to which they went and stayed for relaxation and which by some use became known as a "little white house." I do not recall any that were so used by Eisenhower, Nixon, Ford, Carter, Reagan or Bush. There may be others however about which I do not know.

This made me think that if the vice-presidents established such places they might be designated as "little black houses," but I also know of no such places which any of them has set up.

PICKUP TRUCKS

First time the wide use of pickup trucks was noticed by me was some years back when Ellen and I spent a vacation in the Dakotas. Western farmers and especially Indians love pickup trucks. They usually have four-wheel drives and can easily be maneuvered over the irregular land of the plains and lower hills. You could frequently see owners riding across country, a trail of dust behind, scurrying somewhere without apparently any road bed to follow. I found the joy of a pickup truck when I bought my Meriwether County, Georgia, farm some 15 or so years back. You can haul anything, almost, including dogs, lumber, firewood and supplies in general. I use it all the time. It is a 1983 red, Ford Ranger with a cover over the cargo portion which I had added. I use it all the time in doing things on the farm. I also lend it to my friends. My children use it as an alternative vehicle when their cars are on the blink. Mary Lamar and her daughter, Jane, used it last week and Henry Jr. this week. It is a good truck. It has four-wheel drive into which you can shift. I even lent it to my preacher, Bill Floyd, once when he needed it.

Being a registered redneck I have a pair of plastic dice hanging from the rear view mirror over the dash. The preacher did confess that when he borrowed it he took them down until he returned it. But I am amazed at how many folks come to work every day in pickup trucks. I notice them in the building garage where my office is. I count anywhere from eight to twelve each day, of all makes. Some have covers over the back. These vehicles are comfortable. Mine has a heater, air conditioning, compass, tape player, radio, and ample storage space behind the seat and in the glove compartment. I was quite surprised at this but can understand how those who use them enjoy them and find them less expensive and quite serviceable.

OUT OF SORTS

Riding in a taxi in San Francisco we were going up a steep hill. I wanted to know the name of the hill so I asked the driver what was the name of the hill. His reply was, "I am out of sorts right now and I don't want to talk." So with that I ceased comment and even now wonder what the name of the hill was. It might have been Nob Hill. Another taxi driver just wouldn't stop talking. I started after a while to tell him I was out of sorts and did not wish to talk but refrained as I actually was not out of sorts.

11

Debts and Trespasses

In the Methodist Church in the Lord's Prayer we say, "forgive us our trespasses as we forgive those who have trespassed against us." In some other churches I understand they say, "forgive us our debts as we forgive..." etc. I cannot identify the churches which say debts but I do know the Methodists say trespasses. I am open to being further enlightened, but it seems to me that in praying to God we should not ask to be forgiven of our debt to him. He has created us, has nurtured us and has made us into human beings and we are forever indebted to him for such. I seriously do not wish to be forgiven for that debt. On the other hand, we have almost daily trespassed (i.e. violated) on the laws and rules that God has laid down by which we should live. For such trespasses I do pray to be forgiven and need to be forgiven.

<hr>

HYMNS BY HEART

The Presbyterian Church when I was young had an organization for young folks in the local church which met in late afternoons on Sunday called the Christian Endeavor. The comparable one for Baptists was the BYPU (Baptist Young People's Union) and we Methodists had what we called the Epworth League. I attended the Epworth League every Sunday afternoon late and we sang hymns and had some good times. I am now at the stage in life where the small print in the hymn book is so small I cannot read it. But having been to the Epworth League and having sung these same hymns so often, I find that I have without knowing it actually memorized so many of them from those bygone days that I can sing along with the others in the Sunday congregation without reading the hymn book.

SHARING THE BEST

I like to share the good things in my life with friends. The best thing in my life is my religion. If I did not have a strong belief in God, Christ, and the promises made in the Bible, things would be so much less attractive in this life and I would feel so different. But I have two friends (both men) who, as I assay their attitudes, have no religion in their lives and it distresses me. I think they could be so much happier and have improved outlooks on life here and in the hereafter if they embraced religion in its best aspects. I would not say this to them for they would resent it and it might turn them even more firmly away. But I feel so helpless at being unable to share this great thing with them. Denominationalism is not a part of it but a belief in Christ, God, life eternal, and righteous living is what I am talking about.

THAT'S DIFFERENT

A man asked his preacher (Methodist I am sure) if he would preach the funeral of his faithful old dog. The parson replied, "Who me preach the funeral of a dog?"

The man replied, "Well, I had set aside $500, and $100 would buy his casket and $400 would go to the preacher."

To this the comment of the preacher was, "Well that's different. Why didn't you tell me he was a Methodist Dog?"

A CRAZY IDEA

As you may well know Methodist preachers are moved to another church by the Bishop about every four years. We Methodists believe we should share our bad preachers with others just as we do the good ones. My grandpa Bowden was a Methodist preacher and I checked and found that for a number of years at each of the following places he was the Methodist minister: Augusta, Jonesboro, Fairburn, Senoia, Winterville, Forsyth, Hogansville (where he was when my daddy was born in 1872), Palmetto, Jackson, McDonough and Hartwell. All are in Georgia. His full name was John Malachi Bowden. I suggested to Ellen when our son was born that we name him Malachi in Grandpa's memory. It fell on deaf ears for which I now think Henry Jr. is most grateful. Some guys, such as I, just have crazy ideas and that is all there is to it.

UNCOMFORTABLE DADDIES

I notice at the Christenings in our church when the parents carry the little one to the altar for the ceremony it is usually the daddy who has the infant in his arms and I think how poor a carrier the daddy is. He seems uncomfortable, ill at ease and really doesn't know how. Baby would be much more satisfied if in its mama's arms I am sure, and when the preacher returns the baby to the parents it is usually to mama to whom he gives it; mamas know how. Daddies don't seem to catch on.

I'D SIT AT ALL SITS

When I go to church and sit in my pew with my family along with me, I like to sit there and remain seated. Oh, I don't mind standing for a prayer or an occasional song but otherwise, I like to just sit. Methodists have never been great up and down folks in their services. However, in recent months I have noted that we Methodists are up and down as much almost as my Episcopal friends and I believe they must stand for a greater time than they sit. I counted the number of times we got up and down the other

Sunday and it was a total of six times. Man alive that gets an old man whose knees are not too snappy anyway, but it seems to be the trend. I bet if you named a church instead of "All Saints," just plain old "All Sits," you would get a lot of members from the up and down denominations.

BETTER UNDERSTANDING

It was reported that one of Reverend Ralph Sockman's church members said to him one day, "Dr. Sockman, you just don't know how much you have meant to us. Until you came, we did not know the full meaning of sin."

CUTTING THOUGHTS

Preacher one time came to church with a Band-Aid on his face. He explained to his congregation that that morning he was shaving and got to thinking about his sermon and cut his face. Afterward one of his parishioners said to him, "Parson, let me suggest that next time you think about your face and cut the sermon."

WHAT A JOB

Got to thinking about the life of a preacher. I cannot see how a preacher copes with it. Say this morning he preaches the funeral of a fellow whom he did not even know but is the brother of one of his parishioners. And from that he goes to a place of joy and anticipation in the form of a pre-wedding rehearsal where all is joy, laughter, and light. The next morning he talks to the Women's Missionary Circle (but what would I say at one of those?). And then the meeting of the church board is that night at which he must be able to quote readily all of the church statistics. The next morning he finds himself visiting the sick and lonely. And during all this, he must be working on his Wednesday night service message and the sermon for the next Sunday. Careful he must be not to say what he said last week. That is some schedule and my hat is off to those preachers for they seem to be able to take it in stride and keep the faith themselves.

12

Totally Random

I have about decided that if I had to do it all over again, I would not be a lawyer. I decided that what I would be is a country music songwriter and I've already written my first song, which goes like this:

I got a corn on my lip from kissing you;
I've got a corn on my lip from kissing you.
It's on my upper lip and it surely is a pip;
I've got a corn on my lip from kissing you.

I notice that my corn is turning red;
Could be that it's coming to a head?
I wouldn't change it if I could;
Cause when I look back it was so good.

I got a corn on my lip from kissing you.

MORE COUNTRY MUSIC

As I said before, I have taken up a new vocation of writing country music and the following is my second effort:

I got marrying on my mind from loving you;
I got marrying on my mind from courting you.
It's deep down in my heart and it's been there from the start;
I got marrying on my mind from loving you.

We're going to have a great big house plum full of kids,
There'll be Jane and Sue and Nancy,
And a little guy named Clancy;
And we'll top it off with a great big boy named Bill.

I'm going to pop the question this coming Saturday night;
If your answer is "No," the top of my head off I'll blow.
If your answer is "Yes," I'll be the happiest guy in the world
     I guess.
I'm going to pop the question this coming Saturday night.

BIG-MOUTH FROG

Sometimes it seems to me that I can open my big mouth to my great regret more than anyone I know. I always regret it later but it is too late. This story illustrates the point. There was a bullfrog who lived all his life in Maine and he so badly wanted to spend a winter in Florida but had no way of getting there. So he devised a plan. He had two good friends who were eagles. He told them when they went to Florida to each put one end of a string in his beak and he the frog would clamp down with his teeth on the center of the string and when they took off for Florida he would be in the middle just riding along. This worked well until the eagles were flying over Charing, Georgia. Somebody down there looked up and saw what was going on and exclaimed, "Man, that is a great idea, I wonder who thought that up?"

The frog, impressed with his own ingenuity, opened his big mouth and said, "I did," and that was the end of the frog.

~

A KEEN SENSE OF TASTE

I thank the good Lord often that I have a keen sense of taste as far as I am concerned, but I also thank Him that I do not have what I term a highly discriminating sense of taste. For instance, some folks say, "Man alive, that coffee we just had was awful, wasn't it?" To me it was great. All coffee tastes the same to me whether it is decaffeinated or regular. It is black and hot and welcome usually. My Eunice makes me a pot of coffee when she leaves on Friday afternoon for me to plug in on Saturday morning. I do so and if any is left in the same pot on Sunday morning, I plug it in again and have another cup of the same coffee. It tastes just like the one the day before to me.

I like all foods generally and the only thing that I can easily pass up as not really to my liking is cucumbers. I like them as dill pickles but not as raw cucumbers. I hear some folks for instance say, "That had too much paprika in it, didn't you think?" To which my reply is, "I have no idea what paprika tastes like and it didn't seem to have too much of anything in it to me. It was all good." If your sense of taste is so acute you are in for so many, many disappointments because food did not measure up to your tastes. I have never experienced such.

I have never tasted any bad ice cream.

~

A SQUEEZE OF THE HAND

Big things that happen in my life seem to be the ones that attract the big attention. Such things as birthdays, anniversaries, and the other similar traditional events are what I mean. It is the same with others, I am sure. This is as it should be, for these events mean so much in our lives. I have heard so many say that they just wish to forget their birthday, but I don't really think they mean it. They want the center of the stage at least one day in the year.

But as the years go by these big events and the memories of those special days seem to blend into one general sort of remembrance with the exception of the last one you experienced, which you recall in detail.

I am sure that to me, and I have reason to feel that to many others, the most meaningful things in life, the ones that you remember with greatest vividness and that you think back on over and over and get a warm feeling from, are the little things. Glances across a crowded room, a raising of the eyebrows, a smile of recognition and approval or a pat on the knee in church are the sorts of things I am talking about.

One in particular I recall with great frequency, and one that warms my whole being, occurred some seven years ago now. I was told by my doctors that I was faced with a serious heart problem requiring the replacement of a valve. They were understanding and yet frank. They told me it was a life threatening, high-risk operation. But I was willing because the life the Lord had allowed me to live up to that point had been so very much more than I had deserved and had been so wonderful in my estimation that I felt to ask for any more would be an act of ingratitude. Mind you, I was not anxious to go and very much wanted to live, but those were my feelings.

I had the operation, which lasted some four hours. My heart was disconnected from its blood pumping function and my circulation was sustained by an awesome machine. I had the very finest of surgeons and thankfully I survived the operation.

When I came to I was covered with blankets but was very cold. I was strapped to the table in what was called a recovery room in which intensive care is provided for such cases. I felt alone. I was cold. I was strapped down to the cart on which I had been placed. There was a large tube down my throat making it impossible to speak. I was thirsty yet I was alert to my surroundings. I wondered whether they had found my problem inoperable and whether I had just been placed where I was to await the end. I desperately wanted to talk to someone or to communicate with someone. There was a nurse in attendance upon my needs. She reached down and held my tied-down hand. Her hand clasp was warm and I in an effort to express my thanks to her squeezed her hand as best I could. She seemed to understand and she squeezed my hand again in response. She was black and I was white, but at a time and in a situation like that there is no color. It is one human being, one child of God, speaking by the simple squeezing of a hand a tender feeling of concern and I shall never forget it.

THANKSGIVING THOUGHTS

When you say you "like" something it really means you are actually thankful for it. Some of the great and the trivial things in my life that I like include my morning coffee as I read the morning paper, which I also enjoy; my longtime good and faithful servant and friend, and one whom I held in deepest affection, Eunice Jackson, who was at our house for over 25 years; life, coupled with more than deserved measure of health that has been mine; the practice of law to which I go each day, hoping that as I go the day will enable me to help some other soul in need of help; my co-workers and emphatically my secretary who is great and puts up with much; physical warmth; the ability to speak, hear, see and feel; books and a reasonably active mind enabling me to enjoy them; my friends, without whom life would be mighty gray; my wonderful children and grandchildren; music; travel; my comfortable automobile; my church and my minister; my Christian faith; dogs; flowers; ladies (there is some sort of elegance in feminine companionship); renewal of bodily strength after rest; pleasant smells and odors; Emory University; the orderliness of life and the certainty of death on this old terrestrial ball; and there are so very many more — and yet for all of those I am truly thankful.

WORDS SOMETIMES GET MIXED UP IN FOLKS' MINDS

My daughter Mary Lamar was able to locate a servant who is now with us. She is by no means another Eunice and works but four hours a day.

She says she is an "evangelist" and her husband is a Bishop

in the Holiness Church. It is the second marriage for each; their last name is Dozier. If she attended college I am positive she was not initiated into Phi Beta Kappa. I have been sick with the shingles for several months and unable to go to work.

Each morning the Bishop brings her to work and they suggest that we have prayer. This I welcome and on one morning she placed her hand on my head and among the other things she said was, "Lord you have all of the powder and the glory. Please put your powder on this man, put your powder all over him and Lord please make him well again." I was glad at that point even to get "powdered."

The Bishop (she calls him "Bish") is a tall, gangly man, wears a white-billed cap and is amiable enough. He drives a white Cadillac so I told him to leave it parked in my drive as long as he wished for it would certainly improve my standing with my neighbors.

A DOG STORY

In the early 1970's while on a trip that carried us to Memphis, Ellen and I made the purchase of a dog. Ellen loved dogs even more than I, and I had owned them all my life. It was a black poodle and it was dubbed "Lamb." It was a fine little mutt and survived Ellen, her mistress, by some four years. As the old saying goes Lamb was a fine dog, but she would bite. At 16 years of age this past fall Lamb became ill and was diagnosed as having a heart problem which at age 16 finally brought on death. All of the family loved Lamb and a part of it was because Ellen, the mistress, loved Lamb so much. So we had a dog funeral down in the back yard. Most of the family was in attendance. Mary Lamar got a small white cardboard "casket" and Henry Jr. dug the hole with some help from others in the family who wished to have a hand in it all. Grandchildren Caroline and Henry III made rudimentary crosses from sticks, Mary Lamar brought a flower to lay upon the casket, Henry Jr. filled the hole, providing a small mound on top. Henry Jr. said a short prayer and we all cried a bit. I know some folks do not care for dogs but we in our family love them and they mean a lot to us. I hope they always will.

⁂

HOW DO YOU BEGIN?

I asked an accomplished lady portrait painter the other day where she first touched the canvas with her paint brush when painting a portrait. Her answer was interesting to me. She said that she started with the eyes and got them set as to shape, direction and the like and this enabled her to then bring in the head and its relationship to the whole.

Then I asked a well-known surgeon to tell me when he was going to operate where did he make the first cut. He said it bothered him too and that he sometimes thought about it the night before while in bed and he took about five or six minutes at the time of the operation again to try to determine where he should cut first.

How to begin is important in anything we undertake. But you gotta get started sometime and finally you just get down to it and get the job done. But these two beginnings were interesting to me.

⁂

MEN'S BARBER SHOPS

Never having been in a ladies' beauty salon I have no idea what goes on in there. But averaging about 60 days between trips I have been in lots of barber shops for men and I do know what transpires in those male sanctuaries. The one I go to is a redneck layout on Cheshire Bridge Road at the top of the hill. It has but two chairs. Sometimes both barbers are there and sometimes not. Today, only one was there and I was the only customer. The barber's name, I learned, is Awtry from LaGrange. Said he had run lots of shops. He asked where I lived. I said Buckhead and he said, "You are one of those millionaires." I told him I wanted him to sign an affidavit about that so I could show it to my friends. He got to talking about wives. He allowed they were good to have. They told you when to take out the trash and all that sort of stuff.

As to your hair, he doesn't wash it or shampoo it or curl it. He just cuts it and does that in about 20 minutes for six bucks. He talked about a lot of things in 20 minutes including rebuilding an old wheelbarrow. He wanted to know if I wanted my nose hair trimmed. I told him no. I didn't know I had any. How about your eyebrows he said. I gave a no to that, too. I just wanted my head hair cut and that cut short, and that is what he proceeded to do, I mean.

Said he doesn't smoke, chew tobacco or dip any snuff, for which I was grateful. His whole shop is only about twenty by thirty feet square but it has plenty of parking space and I am glad that I have found another good redneck barber shop since my old one went out of business.

Times have changed but I remember when I was a small boy the fire engine house #12 was not too far from our house. A jovial fireman named Mr. Cottonham would when not fighting fires cut kids' hair for ten cents. Mama would give me a dime and say go up to the firehouse and get your hair cut. I loved to be able to go and see the horses. Mr. Cottonham would say, "Boy, get up here in this chair." It consisted of a regular chair across the arms of which he put a board so I would be high enough for him to work on. He cut it to a fare-thee-well using manual and not electric clippers. They sort of pinched sometimes but it was worth it all just to get to see the horses. At the end of the experience Mr. Cottonham would say, "Boy, I am gonna put some elephant sweat on your head now." What he called elephant sweat was some concoction in a bottle some of which he squirted on my head and combed the hair straight back. Man that stuff did smell. I guess at that age I felt it really was elephant sweat, but I had no idea an elephant smelled like that.

~

CUSS WORDS AND PROFANITY IN GENERAL

I spent five years plus in Uncle Sam's Army and have otherwise not lived exactly what might be termed a cloistered life so I have been exposed to cussing, both plain and fancy, over the years. Let me say first that I don't like it. As has often been said to me it indicates a lack of an otherwise adequate vocabulary. In addition, the words are not attractive.

It is bad enough in the language of men but when the women use it I find it even more abhorrent. I heard one lady recently use language that I don't even believe I heard in the Army. It certainly lowers the lady in the estimation of her hearers.

But how about some of the commonly used cuss words? Take for instance the term "son of a bitch," which is abbreviated SOB. Analyzing it, this is what it seems to me to mean. All female dogs are known as "bitches." Therefore, all male puppies are sons of bitches. Thus, when you call someone by that term you are saying the equivalent of, "you are a male dog." What is so bad about that? I have had some fine sons of bitches in my lifetime, namely Fritz, Spot, Bach, Freckles, P.B., Maypo, Chester, and others. They were all great. Yet, by definition, each of them is a son of a bitch. Many of them had finer traits of character than some humans I have met. So to use that term is not necessarily a term of opprobrium. It is about like saying, "that fellow is a male dog." So what?

My wife and I on several occasions walked out of movies early because of the offensive language heard used, and some of it even by children. Then you take the term, "go to hell." Suppose we substituted for those words the language, "descend to the lower regions." I think for one that such language would create more attention than the one common in use. Then we heard the word "bastard" used as applied to certain persons. A bastard is a person who was born out of wedlock. Suppose we instead of calling someone a bastard simply said, "Certainly his parents were not married." I believe such substituted language as "male dog," "descend to the lower regions" and "certainly his parents were not married" would bring much more emphasis to what the user is trying to suggest than the commonly used language now being so widely employed.

DECISIONS

I look back over my life to see if I have made any significant decisions and I find that I really have. Let me tell you some of them. At first I decided to go to Emory University which has been one of the major contributors in my life. Then I decided to be a lawyer which has been decidedly interesting. Then I got up the courage and decided to ask Ellen Fleming to marry me which she did and from that marriage have come so many blessings.

Then several years ago after I had a small fender bender collision while driving which was clearly my fault, I said to myself, "Bowden, you old goat, you ought not to be driving an automobile," and from that day on I have never driven again. I kept my driver's license because no one ever took it away and I use it for identification.

Not driving does not bother me as it does some people because I feared I might get in an accident that would kill some lady who had a five- or six-year-old child and that child would be deprived of the value of having a mother. Somebody in the group I am going with drives so I find no difficulty in getting where I want to go. But this great decision also brought another valuable thing to my life. It has gotten me to know Wen Mackey who is now my good friend and drives me wherever I wish to go. I could not get along without Wen and I have told him so.

There are other great decisions which I have made such as in 1950 to quit smoking. My argument to myself, which was one-sided of course, went something like this: "Now Bowden, you crazy oaf, you are buying cigarettes which cost money, putting fire to one end of the cigarette and inhaling the smoke, damaging your health. No good is coming to you from it. It is not a good example for your children and the wise decision for you is to straight out quit." I quit that day. I was smoking a package a day, have never smoked one since, have never desired to, have benefited health-wise (although you would not believe it looking at me now), have never wanted any more, and cannot understand some of my friends who are addicts.

There are a number of other decisions you have made of which you are proud but which in your advanced years and limited ability you cannot recall.

NEIGHBORHOODS CHANGE

When I was a boy I knew the names of every one of the neighbors on both sides of the street and on lots of the nearby streets and could identify them on sight. I spoke to them regularly and liked them all.

I got to thinking about it today. I have been living where I now live for 40 years. I know the names of some of the neighbors, but I could not say truthfully that I could identify on sight anyone living in any of the houses on either side of mine nor in any house I could see from my front door. And I feel certain that they could not identify me either. I wonder what has brought on this change. I am sure I would like them if I knew them and I hope they would like me but we never see each other. Our paths do not cross. We go to our daily chores by car and there is no close front-porch sitting and chatting. Maybe sitting inside and TV has helped make this change. Everyone is inside glued to the tube. What a shame this is. I admit I am not a TV viewer. I do not wish to be entertained constantly but prefer to read or do something else. I look at TV not over an average of 3 hours a week. But whatever is causing this change to me, the change is not good.

REFLECTIONS ON CIVIL WAR (WAR OF SECESSION)

Though both my grandfathers fought as Confederate soldiers in the War of Secession (Civil War) from 1861 to 1865, and though I have always been a died-in-the-wool Confederate, yet upon somber reflection I have decided it was a great thing the South lost the war.

In the first place if we had been allowed to secede we would have had two nations here instead of one. It would resemble North and South Korea which is bad. Or even worse East and West Germany. It would have heightened hatreds, inflamed prejudices, and developed intense Northern and Southern nationalistic feelings which would have made the ultimate coming back together again most difficult. Even the Methodist Church, which split into Northern and Southern branches back in the 1850's, didn't get back together until the 1930's.

In the second place, though the war was not supposedly fought over the issue of slavery, nevertheless that was a concern of major importance. Slavery would have continued in the South and from where I now sit it is unthinkable to be able to condone such a practice which promotes one human being being owned by another outright.

Another thing, I am learning to love Yankees with a clearer conscience — but it is a strain.

CONTENTMENT

There is probably no really adequate definition of contentment. It involves many things. I guess one of the elements is the absence of cares, but to continue without cares indefinitely would be terrible as I see it. Cares, concerns, problems, and difficulties are the elements that give zest and challenge to life. The absence of these things would bring on sort of nirvana which to me would be mighty boring. So contentment has got to be a sort of present, temporary but passing thing in its strictest definition. I can think of a situation which produced contentment to me. For instance to be sitting in winter time in my chair by the open wood fire, reading or just sitting and watching the flames while my wife Ellen was on the sofa opposite sewing, reading the paper or also just watching the flames. Our health was good. Our children were leading acceptable, orderly lives and we were free of hovering debt.

There passed between us conversation, comment, or even just plain silence. And just to be there and to know and feel that real love exists each for the other certainly is one situation that can be called contentment.

Then another, if you and she are in your car, it has been tuned up, tires good, weather mild, plenty of gas. You are on a drive to a pleasant destination or to visit some place you have always wished to go or to return to and you have a pleasant place at which to have lunch. This to me also spells contentment. If you add to it an occasional reaching over by either to the other with a pat on whatever spot is appropriate accompanied by an expression that says, "I love you," then the contentment I mentioned is spelled with a capital "C."

THE PIANO

Buying a second-hand piano isn't the easiest thing to do when you are buying it from an individual. My granddaughter Caroline is eight years old and though she may not ever be an accomplished pianist, I still want her to take lessons so she, and we, can know whether she has such talent.

If that is to be done, the first requirement is to get a piano. Since her parents do not have a piano, I felt that the least Grandpa could do was to get one so she would have one available. It also meant that I would get to see her more often since she would be practicing at my house.

So I ran a small ad in the weekly newspaper saying I would pay $350 for a piano for my 8 year old granddaughter to use in taking piano lessons. Friends said you would never find a good piano for that price. It was worth trying. They could not have been more wrong. The phone started ringing the day the ad appeared and some fifteen or more folks were anxious to sell for that sum. In fact, one desperate lady said she did not want the money if I would just come and haul it away.

After many conversations I found one out just beyond Oglethorpe University. I went to see it and it was exactly what I had in mind. It belonged to Mrs. Jane Spiller. I asked her husband if he was any kin to Rell Jackson Spiller, who formerly owned the old Atlanta Crackers. Somehow he had never heard of that Spiller.

Now buying a piano and getting a piano moved are two different things, I promise you. Through the telephone directory I located a piano mover and he met me with his truck at 9:30 on Saturday morning at Oglethorpe and followed me (I was driving my red Ford pick-up truck and was easy to follow) to the Spiller residence where they were expecting us. The name of the piano mover was Charles Ricks. When he emerged from his truck he had one other man with him. I wondered how those two fellows were ever going to get that piano out of the house by themselves. That piano was heavy. I wondered even more and became really concerned when I realized that the second man was totally blind and older than Charles Ricks. But my fears were allayed when I realized that they knew what they were doing and this was by no means the first piano they had ever moved. The truck was well equipped, they had portable ramps and dollies as needed.

Charles Ricks was a fine looking, well built, athletic type fellow who was at least six feet three and looked sort of like a movie star potential. He got on one end and his helper, the blind one, took the other. Charles gave his helper quiet, accurate directions as to what his movements should be and they worked as a team just perfectly together. I paid Mrs. Spiller, and Charles and his helper followed me to my home to carry it into the house. This they did also with the same dispatch shown when they loaded it.

When they had finished the job I asked what the charges would be. It was only then that I learned that the older of the two, the one with the sight deficiency, was the person in charge.

He said the charge would be $90. I told him in anticipation of the cost I had that morning mortgaged my house, had a one hundred dollar bill and wondered if he had a ten. He reached in his pants pocket and handed me a bill and said, "Is that a ten?" I told him it was but that I would like for Charles Ricks to tell him it was for assurance. He said no, that if I said it was a ten that was sufficient. I then handed him the one hundred dollar bill and told him to get Charles Ricks to verify to him that it was. He said no, that if I said it was that was sufficient.

As they prepared to leave I complimented them on their efficiency and pleasantness. It was then that I got the big surprise. Charles Ricks said to me, "You know my helper here is my father."

Well, you know I cry pretty easily anyhow, and this revelation brought tears to my eyes. What a beautiful relationship this was between father and son. The son, a fine specimen of a man with great charm and personality, and the father, limited by lack of vision. But the two of them as a team worked perfectly together with gentleness of voice and action and with complete understanding and obvious affection between the two. I tell you I was impressed.

As they prepared to leave the elder Mr. Ricks told me the piano needed tuning and that if he could help me he would do so. I found out that not only do he and his son move pianos but he also tunes them. This made me think back to earlier years in my own childhood home and our piano which also had to be tuned occasionally. I seem to recall that the piano tuner then was also blind. I figured that loss of sight must require of an individual that he rely more than others on hearing, making their hearing more acute. I told him that by all means I would wish for him to be the person to tune it.

So, on Monday morning I called the Ricks' home. His wife, a really nice lady, answered and said he was not in, he was teaching. I asked what he taught and I got my second big surprise. She said he teaches American history at Clayton Junior College. I inquired as to where he got his training to teach and she told me he had been graduated from Mercer University then attended Yale and was now at work on his Ph.D. degree at the University of North Carolina. What a fellow and what a man. He never gave in to adversity and rose above it to marriage, two fine sons, a wonderful education, and the full respect of his community. My hat is off to him and his family.

He returned from teaching and called me and he is to come tomorrow and tune my piano. His daughter will bring him. I asked him how long he had been without sight and he told me he was born that way. He said his mother had measles while she was pregnant with him and that the side effects resulted in his loss of sight. All this serves only to cause me to bemoan my own meager accomplishments with all of the wonderful advantages that have come my way. Mr. Ricks did come, with his daughter, and he tuned the piano well. So, it is now ready for use by my wonderful grand-daughter, Caroline Bruton Bowden, when she begins taking piano I hope this fall.

⤙⤚

LADIES' SHOES AND THE GOSPEL

My longtime good friend and fellow Emory Trustee, Bishop Bevel Jones, visited me while I was recently a patient in the Emory Hospital. He told me that when an undergrad at Emory he needed money to help pay his expenses and he got a job in a ladies' shoe store in downtown Atlanta. He said the bigger the lady, the smaller she wanted her shoes to be. On one Saturday afternoon he was trying to get a too small pair on a too large lady and working hard at it. Now Bev since early infancy has had no hair. In plain language he is bald headed. While he was working away, head bobbing up and down, the lady whose eyesight was not too good looked down, saw his bald head moving vigorously, and she thought it was her own knee. So she quickly picked up her skirt and threw it over Bev's baldness to his great surprise.

I said, "Bev what did you do?"

He said, "I offered up a short prayer in which I said, 'Oh Lord, if you will just get me out of this dilemma I will preach the Gospel.' He answered my prayer and I have been preaching the Gospel ever since."

⤙⤚

PLAQUES

When someone receives some sort of honor it has become customary to present to her or to him a plaque to hang on the wall. One person I know well has what he calls a "rogue's gallery" upstairs at his home where hang pictures of his grandparents, parents and children at the various points of their development. Also, he keeps the family plaques there such as his daddy's college diploma and other such. This is to me a good idea. Somehow to hang them in a prominent place seems a bit egotistic. They are really for family pleasure and enjoyment and not for general consumption. The public is seldom interested but the family is usu-

106

ally filled with interest about their own family members. Ivan Allen on retirement as Mayor of Atlanta gave to each of his main department heads a caned rocking chair from his office with a small plate on the arm telling of it and that was an extremely nice thing to do.

HOMECOMING

Each October about the middle of the month the Methodist Church at Raleigh, Georgia, near Woodbury has a homecoming. They had it this year on October 17 and I went. My grandpa Bowden (John Malachi Bowden) was born there and that is why I was included in those invited. What a delightful time we had. After considerable talking in the churchyard before services began we had the sermon and that was followed by "eating on the grounds." If you don't know what that term means you ought to go to one. The ladies cook up and bring to the church such food as you have never seen. It would back any of these Atlanta bakeries off the road. Vegetables, salads, pies, cakes, bread, pickles, ham, chicken, beef, pineapple, and you name it. They had it. I went with my cousin Joe Bowden who lives at Luthersville. My children were away from town and could not go. You know how in lots of church services they call the little children to the altar and they get a little child's message. At our Atlanta church the teacher might say something as a starter like this, "How many of you have ever had a birthday?" They would all hold up their hands. Well at Raleigh the teacher said this, "How many of you know what a heifer is?" The quick response was, "It's a cow." Now, if that question had been asked at my church not a hand would have been raised I am certain but down in Raleigh they know right off. They each probably had one or two in their "cow lot" or in the pasture. It all depends, I guess, on what you have been exposed to.

SOME OF LIFE'S GREATEST ASSETS

I have figured out to my own satisfaction that among the wonderful things about life are these. First, I guess memory is the greatest. If you could remember nothing you would be completely lost. Each moment would be a new thing and you would not survive for long without some help. You wouldn't know to eat, to dress, to do anything that comes so wonderfully with memory. Another great element is family. They don't always live up to one's greatest hopes but they are still family, close by kinship, and usually loved with enduring affection. Then along come friends. What great assets they are. As for me, they are I guess my greatest capital asset in that through the friends I have, I feel I have become "rich." Don't forget eyesight either and hearing is also high on the list. If you have lived with or had any close connection with anyone who cannot hear, you can understand how important it is. Another thing. This is true for widows and widowers especially. There is a need to touch someone. I don't mean it in any sordid or improper way but when you have for many, many years been close with your wife or husband so that just to hold one's hand is reassuring and comforting and suddenly no longer do you have anyone to hold hands with, it is something you miss. It signifies understanding, tolerance, and companionship. Everybody needs it as I see it.

13

Funerals and Cemeteries

I t used to be that each church had beside it, convenient to the sanctuary and on flat ground, a cemetery where members of the church could be buried. That was a good custom and the presence of the cemetery added sanctity to the church grounds and made it a place to which families of the deceased could return from time to time even though they moved to far distant points. Except in country areas this is no longer a common practice. I wish it would begin again as a practice.

Last month I visited at Old Bethesda Methodist Church down in Meriwether County. I saw the graves of some of my forebears way, way back. If they were buried at Westview or some other tremendous burial ground, I would probably never visit them. One of the old geezers was named Josiah Bowden, his wife Pollie Ann Murphy, and another John M. and his wife Elizabeth Leamon Akers Bowden.

I have found a cemetery on my farm with only one stone that has an engraving on it. He was Charles Moore and he died in 1888. He was 72 years old. The other tombstones are made of just old field rock with no inscription on them. How I would like to know what went on at the place in these days and just who the descendants of these buried folks are so I could show them the cemetery. I looked up the law on cemeteries and believe me you are dealing with dangerous stuff if you mess with them. So I am leaving the graveyard strictly alone. If I don't they might rise up on a full moon one night and haunt me.

SMALL TOWN FUNERAL

The 95-year-old mother of one of my close friends died the other day after a long illness. I went to the funeral and it brought back wonderful memories. The morning funeral was held in the chapel of the Methodist church and was well attended, followed by the graveside services at the local cemetery. There were lots of family members present from out of town as well as the children and the grandchildren of the deceased. Her son and his wife at their beautiful home had arranged lunch for all out of towners and family. I was privileged to be included and it was something. Family members got to see each other and talk; non-family members were taken right in as if they were family; every conceivable food was provided from salad right on through dessert. What gracious hosts they were and what a good time their friends and family enjoyed being together even under such circumstances. It made me feel that we are wrong when we say all the old values and customs are gone. That is certainly not so and this was a great demonstration of that fact.

FUNERAL SURPRISES

Surprises abound at funerals and as you get older you attend more of them. You get some shocks at most of them. One thing is you see folks there whom you did not realize even knew the deceased. Again, you are surprised at who some of the pallbearers are. Then a lot of the time the things that are said about the deceased don't always stack up with your best recollection of the fellow. But you never know. He might have had some good qualities about which you are not really informed. They have now started a custom of having a preacher read the Bible and recite the Lord's Prayer and other appropriate passages and then to have someone not even always a preacher to be the "eulogist" which means the person who tells you some personal facts about the life of the deceased. Also, seldom does the corpse resemble in the slightest the deceased as you recalled him. Maybe that is good. Depends on how he looked in life.

DIFFERENT FUNERALS

Somehow not until today had I ever attended a Jewish funeral. One of my good friends died last Friday and today (Monday) I attended his funeral. It was a beautiful but a different service from those to which I was accustomed. In the first place all of the Jewish men in attendance wore yarmulkes (the small skull cap covering the crown of the head). I have made diligent effort among my Jewish friends to ascertain the origin of the custom of wearing these but have never had anyone tell me authoritatively about it. They simply say, "Well, it is an old custom." The funeral parlor was packed. The service opened with a cantor singing a funeral song in Hebrew (I was told). His voice was not of operatic caliber and I understood none of the words, but it was a significant thing and not a bad way to get a service underway. The rabbi spoke in Hebrew which I could not understand. Then he read from the Old Testament in English. There were on one or two occasions responses from the combined audience, but I did not know what the responses said. Then the second rabbi delivered a eulogy about the deceased. It was a beautiful thing, well done, giving highlights of the life and family of the deceased. Following this the cantor sang again. Then the pallbearers and the family marched out followed by the rabbi reciting the 23rd Psalm in English. The rabbi also announced the times of what was termed the Shiva which apparently is the times of each day for 8 days when the family will be at home to receive those who wish to come by and visit to show their sympathy. It was an impressive ceremony.

KEEPING CEMETERIES CLEAN

After the death of a loved one, how often folks pledge to themselves that they are going to improve the cemetery lot — make it look nice and clean and green, put a rock or cement border around it and make it a more attractive place for loved ones buried there. But alas, we don't carry out too well our plans. I took the bull by the horns the other day. I got a man to put Zoysia sod on our plot at Oakland and it looks just great after all the rain we have been having. It now has eliminated the self-criticism I experienced earlier on nearly every visit I made. Try it and see if you feel, as it makes me feel, better.

A FIRST IN FUNERALS

Went to a funeral of a friend the other day at the Methodist Church. The service was normal as I had observed funerals over the years until the two preachers had finished their eulogies. Then the deceased having in life been a Thirty-Third Degree Mason, the Masonic Lodge brethren took over and conducted what I assumed was a standard Masonic service. It was nice and not in any way objectionable but it was different. The pallbearers and other service participants wore aprons. They were small ones extending down only to just about the knees and I take it are symbolic of the sort of apron masons in earlier years wore at work to keep the cement and mortar off their britches. They held log pole standards at each end of the casket. One member recited some liturgy and on the casket they placed several items including an apron, a green twig and other objects with a short explanation as to the significance of each. Upon the conclusion of the service, they all marched out following the casket and the family then followed them out of the church. I am sure that to most folks this is not new but I had never seen one and it was educational to me. I am not a Mason nor a member of any other similar fraternal group but I honor those who are in their efforts and this is not written in criticism but simply to relate something I had not known of nor of course ever seen before.

MY WISHES

Of late lots of people I know have desired to have their bodies cremated at death and their ashes strewn over an area to which they were attached during life such as the back yard, at home someplace, at the lake, an area of the ocean, or some other spot which they love. It is my preference to be buried as has been the custom for many, many years. I want to be buried in the Oakland Cemetery in Atlanta, Georgia, right beside my wonderful wife, Ellen. There will not be, beside my family, over two or three people who will witness the burial but that is what I want and I know my family will carry out my wishes. Thank goodness it is everybody to his own wishes in this sort of thing.

14

Living Alone

When after long, happy years together a man loses his wife in death, life becomes a whole new ball game in lots of ways. Where you used to sit together, talk, go over events of the day of each spouse, plan events together, trips, meals, visits, and such, this no longer takes place. So much of the joy of life has gone and you find yourself with lots more time on your hands which is uncommitted and "free" time that you have to readjust your approach to living to handle it. With the new-found time you have you find, if you are willing to do so, that you can get a lot of things done you had been meaning to do but never got around to during your happy married life. If you are endowed, as I have luckily been, with a reasonably good supply of energy and have retained some measure of good health, you seem to work yourself, both at your office and at your home solitude, so as to accomplish things you never imagined you would ever get around to. But all this to me beats by a long shot sitting and "being entertained" by staring almost continually at a not too entertaining television. It is a real change of pace. Sometimes it is faster but by no means is it better than when "she" was with you.

SOUNDS IN THE NIGHT

At night when you are just sitting alone at home and all is quiet a sudden noise is sometimes startling. Often it is the contracting of floor joints which have expanded in the heat of the day and are in the cool of the night contracting again. But the sharpness and loudness of the noise is of course startling to one sitting alone in quietness. That is understandable.

Then the sound of an automobile coming into your driveway late at night is disturbing. What is it? What do they want? You become apprehensive and alerted. Also, when the phone rings at your home after ten o'clock at night it is nearly always calculated to make you feel there must be some emergency somewhere or they would not be calling you that time of night and you are almost afraid to answer the phone.

One of my preachers used to call me at 10:30 at night. It scared the willie out of me. I told him that my parents were old and I was afraid when I got such a late night call something may have happened to one of them and to please call me earlier in the future. It did not register at all. He would call the same time at night again and again.

I have a large mantel clock on the dresser in my own bedroom which ticks and tocks alternately all night long. I love it. It is a homey, reassuring sound to me but when my grandchildren spend the night at Grandpa's house they say it disturbs them. Of course, I do not wind the part of the clock that tolls the hour for that would even bother me. But you know to me a clock ticking with strict regularity such as that is homey sounding and reassuring since, for instance, when thunder and lightning storms come up in the night the clock on the dresser is not affected in the least. It pays no attention and just keeps on with its regular ticking and tocking and you feel that even in the storm all's right with your little world.

THINGS THAT REMIND YOU OF THE DEPARTED

I have noticed that in some instances where a death occurs the surviving wife or husband moves, does away with things that "remind" them of the departed, and seems to start all over. This is strange to me. I have gone through this. I feel just the opposite. I want to have around me the things that remind me of my wife who died in 1986. I loved her devotedly. I do not want to forget anything about her. To me she was perfect. For instance we slept in beds side by side. I still keep her bed made up as it was when she was here. I keep her bathroom glass (a cut glass one) where she had it (mine is plastic). I frequently drink my coffee in the morning from her cup.

The furniture is still arranged as she had it. A gift she gave me way back even before we were married over 50 years ago which was a shaving kit for toothpaste, razor, and the like I still carry though it is taped up, new closure on it, stained with shaving lotion and other substances. Unless there was treachery, divorce, unpleasantness, or some other influencing factor I fail to see why a person, long married, would not want all that he or she could have that would remind them of their departed spouse. I hope I never forget her and what she meant to me and contributed to my life.

WIDOWS AND WIDOWERS

As bad as it is for anyone to lose his or her wife or husband to death, I do believe the life of widows is more restricted than that of widowers. It will soon be five years since my dear Ellen died. They have been tough years. But I have been far freer to do things I would like to do than she would have been had I been the first to die. I miss her terribly, something awful and there have been and still are a lot of tears. But liking to travel and especially by automobile I have been able to drive long distances by car to such places as Key West, Palm Beach, and many other places. I went alone because it is hard to get a companionable other person to go along. I have made trips to other cities by plane such as St.

Louis, Seattle, Washington D.C. and the like. They are pleasant trips, all by myself, but they would have been immeasurably more pleasant and enjoyable had she been my companion. Alas, it just couldn't be. But at least I could go with no fear or trepidation. She, had she survived me, could not have done these things.

Also widows cannot go out to dinner in the evening alone. They are more or less curtailed in their nocturnal activities unless accompanied by some gentleman. I asked a widow why she and another widow or two did not arrange to go out together on these evenings or trips. Her reply was that it just wasn't as much fun, and I guess that is so. It seems unfair that this situation should exist. Even though at 81 (this month) I have no romantic interests nor concerns about remarriage. Yet there is a certain elegance that goes along with feminine companionship and I do enjoy my occasional forays to dinner and so forth with the ladies. They are great! The ladies I am sure find no romantic interest in me. But I do like an occasional hug and a pat. I like hugging and patting.

YOUTH AND OLD AGE

Some fellow the other day who had lost his wife by death some while back stated that on occasion he has the privilege of going out on a "date" with a lady who also is without a spouse. Another guy asked him, "What in the world do you talk about in such a situation?" His response was that when he was in his youth, he and his "dates" talked about a lot of things such as each other, the physical aspects of things, sports events, dances, outings, and other such youthful trivia. Now he said they still talk about the physical aspects of things but they relate it to what medicines each is taking, are they helping you, how are you coming along with your weight-watchers diet, do your ankles swell up at the end of the day, do you sleep well at night, and when you get up in a hurry from a sitting position, do you feel dizzy. And did I tell you the funny thing that happened the other day when they were checking my heart pacemaker? And another side is that when I was younger I could put my right leg through my pants and balance on the right foot while I put the left leg through with no trouble, but not so now. Once I get my right leg through I have to hold on to something to get my left one through. Too many birthdays I guess it is.

All of these subjects are just as vital as the ones talked about as youngsters but they are quite a bit different. Conversation follows the lines of interest and the interests of the older group are surely different. He also volunteered that when he goes out he does not now have to leave the light burning so as to aid him when he gets home because most of the time he gets home before dark.

FACING THE NEW AND UNEXPECTED

When you lose your wife through death and you have had a long, happy life together and you face living alone for the remainder of your life, the prospect is certainly not inviting nor is it in a way challenging. Yet, in another, it is. There is really, I think, no relationship in life equal to that between man and wife, a happily married couple. When death terminates the marriage, the survivor is usually lost in myriad problems, memories, and feelings of regret and self-incrimination. Facing living alone is a new and unexpected thing for which you had not really prepared yourself, particularly when her death was sudden. In advanced years, a second marriage is not attractive nor welcome to most. There can really be no substitute for a great spouse. The establishment of understanding and relationships with the family of the second wife constitutes a major problem in readjustment. Thus, living alone is usually the answer. Initially, it is bad. It gets better as time passes if you retain any degree of reasonably good health. Finally you get used to it and sort of tolerate it and maybe enjoy it, though it is never preferable to the life you had with your spouse. At least you do not have to consult others about your plans for the day or for the foreseeable future. You adopt a routine that is not desirable but is acceptable and your friends make life pleasant for you

119

in innumerable instances. I am not advocating it, by any means, but I am saying that it need not be entirely a state of misery if you will take a mental inventory and make adjustments to meet the change head-on.

15

Getting Older

Notice I did not say "getting old," but "older." I have been old for a long time now. But I have noticed that among my contemporaries getting older and older brings on some rather common bonds of approaches to life. For instance, I turned 84 on July 23, 1994. I use a cane or walking stick as we used to call it. So many of my friends do the same. We call it the "Cane Gang," but don't knock them. They are great aids in maintaining balance, going up and down stairs and perambulating in general. I have a number of them and keep them in my car, at my office, at home, and lots of other places. I leave them places from time to time and have learned never to place them on top of my car. I invariably drive off and that cane is still there but gone when I arrive where I am headed.

Some of my close friends use walkers, wheelchairs, elevators on the stairways in their homes and other such useful aids. I don't recall my daddy using one. He died at 83. My wife's father also died at 83 and he had a number of canes which I have come into ownership of and am using with nostalgic feelings about him.

MORE ON THE CANE GANG

The only redeeming feature of having to use a cane is that you get to park in the handicap zone. But let me say here and now that these canes are great things. They support you when and where you need support. You can goose folks in the back with them and lots of other things. But there has developed for me a sort of code to follow and this is as far as I have gotten with it thus far:

(1) Get one that is the right height for your height.

(2) When seated in a restaurant or elsewhere do not lean it against the wall as it will invariably slide down on the floor.

(3) When seated at a table put it lengthwise under the table.

(4) When stairs have banisters use the cane in one hand and hold on to the banisters with the other.

(5) When sitting in a chair try to get one with two arms. It is much easier to rise when you can push up from both sides.

(6) Avoid getting down on the floor on your knees to do anything as it is mighty difficult to get up again from such position and some have found it necessary to crawl on hands and knees for long distances to find some place on which they can push up with both arms.

(7) Be sure and equip your cane with a rubber tip as otherwise the end is awful slippery and may cause you to fall to your extreme discomfort. Three or four times for me thus far.

(8) Have several canes and keep one in each room and one extra one in each of your automobiles, both the Stutz and the Apperson Jack Rabbit.

(9) Avoid having to step over something regardless of how low it may be. If possible, walk around it.

There are several others I may add later but this is about all your mind can sustain at this point and let it suffice.

For years for some reason we had been gathering odd canes at my home. They now come in handy. There must be 15 or more. Some have gold heads and have been equipped with inscriptions. On one appears this: "A token of esteem for Mr. J.B. Papy on his retiring from J.R. Kanf M. Company. His clerks, August 1st, 1887." And on another this: "From Sergie Munden, Canadian R.F.A. To Dad, 1915." And yet on another this appears: "Stole from D.W. Kemp, Birmingham, Jan. 4th, '89." If these mean anything to anyone reading this I will gladly turn the cane over to them.

STILL MORE: START A CANE COLLECTION NOW

I used to watch some guys using canes or as we used to call them "walking sticks" and I said, "Look at that old goat. He don't need that cane. It is all for the effect."

Man was I wrong. I find the cane to be of unusual use and value in maintaining my equilibrium. I had fallen several times but now feel much more secure with the cane and I am all for their use. It gives you some sort of confidence that without the cane is lacking. I hope you don't reach the cane age but if you do you will find it a tremendous aid. I have a special cane from somewhere that has a brass duck head at the handle and I call it my "Sunday go to meeting" cane so I use it in going to church. There are some fancy ones. Start a collection now and it will be ready for you when "that time" arrives.

MEMORY LOSS

Many of us, as we grow older, lament the loss of memory that makes names, events, details and such, elusive in efforts to recall them. We call it loss of memory. That is, to me, not a good term to really describe it. My theory is the "bushel basket theory," which simply likens a person's memory to a large bushel basket of the type peaches were at one time packed in for shipment. At birth, each of us has such a memory basket. As we have our experiences, each such experience goes into the basket. We can easily retrieve most of them on call. But when the years pile up on us, our baskets get full to overflowing. It is often that we can go back and recall incidents that happened years ago but cannot recall what happened last week. Thus, I say, demonstrates the use of the term "bushel basket." At some point in each person's life, his basket gets full and the incidents that are taking place are thrown on top and most of them fall off and cannot be retrieved. I will be 80 years old in another five or six weeks. My son will be 41 in another six or eight weeks. His basket is half full whereas, mine is now overflowing. Ask me what happened in high school or college and I can tell you pretty quickly but, ask me what happened last month or last year and, so very often, I just cannot tell you the answer.

THINGS I NOTICE IN THESE DAYS

(a) I cannot hear worth a toot; (b) I cannot see worth a hoot; (c) I walk unsteadily; (d) I drop nearly everything I pick up at least once; (e) When I put something on a table it often slides off meaning the surface slants or I didn't get it on properly to start with; (f) I can remember remote things from way back say in childhood but memory fails me often as to more recent events; (g) My appetite is not what it once was but I like ice cream just as much as ever; (h) My desire to do things does not match up with my physical ability to get them done; (i) I sleep more poorly at night but want to lie down more frequently in the day time; (j) I am not what I think I once was either mentally, emotionally, or physically.

But, I am not yet dead, enjoy my friends even more, have more middle of the night interruptions, and can't wait for tomorrow to see what is gonna happen then.

I say to myself every day such things as, "Keep on going, boy. Don't give up. You can beat those post-shingles excruciating pains if you live long enough. You may live longer if you just keep on keeping on as long as you can." It has worked so far.

OLD FOLKS FALLING

There is a tendency that increases with advancing age to lose one's balance, or stumble and to fall or almost do so. I go up two flights of stairs to get upstairs at my house to go to bed. Each has eight steps and every time I climb them I count the steps to make sure I have gotten to the bottom or the top. I have decided that what makes a person (me) have trouble with steps is that you do not move your foot forward enough when coming down and your heel catches on the edge of the steps you are leaving. The going up problem is that you do not lift your foot high enough to be level with the next step and you as a result stumble against the step you are ascending. Now all this applies only to what my son refers to as "you octos" which means the group of folks in their 80's (eighty years old or more). I think often whether I could if I tried do some of the things I did as a youngster and among them are skate and ride a bicycle and I believe I could do the latter but not the former.

***

ACUPUNCTURE

This month marking the first full year that I have been suffering from the very painful and depressing disease of shingles, I decided to try acupuncture. Let me tell you what has happened so far. The acupuncturist, Dr. Yung Fong Soong, is the head of outpatient anesthesiology at the Emory Clinic. She, as you have by now deduced, is of Chinese origin and a very nice fine lady I found out. She also administers acupuncture. When I went to see her the first time she asked a lot of medical questions and then told me that acupuncture only works about fifty percent of the time. I was willing to try it at any percentage since nothing else had helped.

You lie down upon a bed already arranged. You disrobe only to expose the places where your shingles are. Mine were in my head so I only had to take off my hat — easy. The first needle was placed in the extreme upper part of my left ear, the next on the back of my right hand, the third on my right ear, and the fourth on my left hand. Then two or three were placed on my forehead and scalp. I lay on the bed for 30 minutes and then was told to get up and carry on normal activities.

The needles did not hurt when inserted. They did not go straight down in but parallel to the surface and went in about one-half inch. I could hardly feel any of them either going in or being withdrawn. The needle is about two inches long and that includes a round silver handle. The needle is much smaller than the needle used in flu shots and the like. When withdrawn there was no bleeding and no Band-Aids applied. There was absolutely no pain connected with it that I felt.

Dr. Soong, I learned, has a 21-year-old son, college graduate, now in Indonesia where he teaches English in the morning and studies Chinese in the afternoon. His mama, Dr. Soong, has absolutely no wrinkles and appears to be no more than 25 years old herself. She and her nurse, Marcie Price, were both just as nice as could be. They answered all questions directly. They would not allow me to take their picture nor bring home a needle to show friends. I asked Dr. Soong if her maiden name was Fong and she married a Soong. She said no. She was married to a Dr. Holzman, who teaches pharmacology at Emory Med School.

All medical personnel at the Emory Clinic hold her in high regard for acupuncture is only one of her activities. After five treatments as described above I was advised to call them again in two months, and if no progress was reported they would reschedule me for further examination and possible treatment. Thus far, I have experienced no results either favorable or unfavorable. I am glad to have tried it. I am exhausted from the effects of the ailment and will try voodooism if it offers any possible hope.

GETTING UP IN YEARS

Today (7/23/91) I turned 81. Somehow I don't feel a day over 80. I have noted some good and bad symptoms. The bad ones are I am walking more slowly, talking more slowly, get tired a lot more easily, have far less energy than formerly, have a much increased lack of balance, like to hold on to the railing when going up the steps or down, my hearing is impaired and I have two hearing aids, my eyesight is poorer and have had two cataract operations, and want to take naps much more frequently than formerly. But there are good things too, which include no quavering in the voice, retention of at least some facial expression, good teeth, can still drive my car with ease (drove 183 miles last Saturday), am not stooped over, can carry a full cup of coffee from the breakfast room to the back porch without spilling a drop, and can get in and out of the bathtub unassisted. And there are others.

One thing I am thankful for is that I have not degenerated into an "old grouch" like several in my acquaintance have. They seem to take joy in complaining about everything that comes up. We, as I see it, have far too few days left to spend them in grousing about everything. I like affirmative, upbeat, happy, optimistic approaches. If something is bad, just keep quiet about it. If something is good, give voice to it. Others very definitely do not enjoy being in the company of chronic grouches.

LIKE FATHER, LIKE SON

Though he never to my knowledge had any heart trouble, I used to see my father while seated sometimes on the porch or in the living room at night holding his finger on his wrist and counting his pulse. I used to say to myself, "What in the world makes Daddy do that?" Yet the other night I caught myself doing the very same thing. In fact I did it twice. Now I have had heart disorders including a pig valve and a pacemaker. Each thus far is percolating well the medics say and that is as good as one might ask for. However, I have so many times heard when a man has died this statement: "Well, you know, he was just at his doctor's office last week and the doctor said he was doing fine and in good health for his age."

But then death holds no horror for me. It is coming and I cannot avoid it. I don't want it to hurry but when it does come I want to be as prepared for it as possible and the best way to do that I feel is to keep as close to the good Lord as possible and don't worry or dread it.

Remember also the words of the old lament, "When you're in the ground six feet deep, no more fried chicken will you eat." And I do like fried chicken.

THE DOMINANT HICKEY

As nearly everyone in hearing distance knows by now, I am in the throes of about every kind of illness you can name. I am going to the dermatologist for the horrible shingles. It is on the left side of my cranium and aches continuously. Bumps appear and some seem more determined than others. There is one that when you touch it is to set off the entire scalp in paroxysms of pain. The doctor asked me whether or not I wished him to freeze it with liquid nitrogen. He referred to it as something like "the controlling lesion" but that may be wrong. I said no for I was not sure what might result. The next time out I told him to go ahead and freeze the dominant hickey which he did and I can see no difference. But I heard him out in the hallway talking to a conferee and he said, "You know, Mr. Bowden refers to the controlling lesion as the dominant hickey," and from that I got an echo of some mirth among the medics.

If any of you have any suggestions about how to recover, please let me know. My latest is a pair of Chinese health balls, somewhat smaller but approaching a golf ball in size. Carry them in your pocket and hold them and rub them together as you walk. (Footnote — I still have the shingles as before.) I am also each morning drinking a tablespoon of cod liver oil mixed with skim milk which is reported to improve one's eyesight. I still cannot see as well as when I was in high school. I take more pills than Vitamin Flintheart but they have not helped the situation as I appraise it.

DOCTORS ARE THOROUGH AND I MEAN THOROUGH

Been losing weight unexplainedly so I went to a great doctor the other day and I mean doctors today are thorough. At least this one was. Let me tell you some of the things "we" did. I say we because he and his assistants were doing it and I was cooperating to a degree. Reviewed medicines now being taken, took blood pressure, thumped and listened to heart beat with stethoscope (130 over 80), took six blood samples, checked weight, asked numerous questions, had me an enema (what a joyful thing), electrocardiogram, urinalysis, x-rayed me in chest and abdomen, made what I call a thorough proctologic examination (one of life's great experiences if you have not already found that out) and had me provide a 24-hour collection in order to do further urological tests. At this juncture I have not heard what my life expectancy is but since I turn 82 this month, I know the time is drawing short.

But man alive who would have had it better than have I. I would be the biggest ingrate in the world if I complained about not having any more of it since what I have had this far has been so terrific to me.

IT'S GONE

Let me tell you something, boys, it's gone! And you may say, What's gone? And I tell what's gone is modesty. Having been in the hospital on other occasions, I knew that the nurses would bring me a urinal and say, "When you have finished, let me know and I'll come."

You can forget that. They bound into the room with the urinal and say, "Big H, let's get going!"

They stand next to you holding your back to keep you from falling. They are able faithfully to point the pointer and locate the opening in the urinal. Sometimes it's a little more difficult than others and I wonder whether the hole of the urinal is getting smaller or the pointer is getting larger. I assure you it's not the latter, which hasn't happened in 35 to 40 years. But just count on it fellows; it's a whole new ball game and you are going to play first base. When you go to the bathroom, they accompany you and carefully see that you are back in bed afterwards. I've got two nurses that work twelve hour shifts each day and the number one nurse that I have is named Bettie Willis. It's awfully important that you get a good one and I surely have.

A FAMILIAR FACE

I presented a check to the teller at the branch of the national bank located in the lobby of the building in which my office is located. Seeing that she was a new teller and wanting to be helpful, I said, "I guess you will wish to have some identification."

She was cute as a button and she looked up at me and said, "Oh, no, I won't need any identification. My grandma knows you."

SAGE ADVICE

When you have begun to use a walking stick and you come to an obstacle which you may either step over or go around, by all means go around it. You will avoid falls that way.

Robert Browning wrote the following:

Grow old along with me!
The best is yet to be,
The rest of life, for which the first was made...

Obviously old RB had not gotten there, for such has certainly not proven to be a sound observation. It should be about like this:

Grow old along with me!
The worst is yet to be,
The time of life for which the earlier years
have not prepared you.

FINALE

If I live until December 28 of this year [1993], I will have lived as long as my father lived, 83 years, 5 months and five days. Let me suggest you take the time to write down as I have the important dates in your family background. The dates of birth and death of parents, grandparents and as far back as you can go. These facts are interesting and bring out some things that please you and on the other hand some things you had just as soon forget about those old geezers. But once they were young geese just as you think you now are. Think again.

IT MAKES YOU WAKE UP

Over about the 15th chapter of Ezekiel in the Bible is a story about some Jewish folks who were taken captive and lived among the heathens on the River Chebar, wherever that was. Some of their friends, or at least old Ezekiel, went down to visit them and this is about what he says along about the 15th verse: "I went down to see them on the River Chebar and remained seven or eight days and was astonished." This brought to mind that before this terrible shingles deal I am going through I used to see guys, close friends like George Craft, walking with a cane and struggling to arise from a chair or get into or out of an auto and I said to myself, "Man alive, it can't be as bad as he makes it out to be. He could do better than that I bet."

He was in exile on the river Chebar and now I have visited him there for longer than seven days and he has my every sympathy because he wasn't putting on a bit. It is tough and I now see things through his eyes — the eyes of experience — and I know he is legitimate in his complaints and his disability. My heart goes out to him and others in the same shape that had not been the case previously. It is pretty easy to criticize others for seeming fakery but when you experience it yourself you know far better and your criticism turns into full knowledge and you want no more part of the river Chebar.

My apologies to all who I thought might be overdoing it just a bit.

WHEN YOU HAVEN'T SEEN THEM IN A LONG TIME

Have you noticed that sometimes someone introduces you to a person, gives their name and you realize, "What the heck, I knew that guy or that lady years ago." And so often the years have exacted such a toll you just plain don't recognize them. Somebody says, "Henry, you remember old Esau Doolittle, I know." And indeed I do but this don't look like the Esau Doolittle of years back. He has no hair, has an enormous paunch, wears thick glasses. You just plain would not have known him.

And the same thing is true of the ladies. They have turned gray or have dyed their hair some odd-ball color, have become "plump" never "fat." They wear easy-walker shoes whereas when you last saw them they had on dancing pumps. These changes are a fact of life but they are real shockers sometimes. Even on occasion you see some old goat you knew in college and doggone it they don't seem to have changed a bit. They look just like they did back then. I don't understand it but some folks are just that way. But the saddest of all are the members of the old crowd who so much resist change that they dye everything dyeable, paint everything paintable, refuse to buy a hearing aid, and go through the period of advancing years fooling nobody but themselves. I believe we ought to act, be, and look our ages, as tough as it is. You might as well get with it because it has surely gotten with you.

REDUCED ENERGY LEVEL

Somehow all my life thus far my energy level has been high. At most anytime day or night I have been ready and able to go. Somehow the tide is turning. I find myself ready but not nearly as able to go as previously. I can't figure it out. What in the world happened? I get 8 or 9 hours in bed every night (not all of it sleeping because my nocturnal rest is interrupted not infrequently) but when I get up in the morning about 7:15 and eat a modest breakfast, I have the urge to lie down again and rest. Rest from what? Haven't been doing anything and normally I would be charging off to the daily battles. But, alas. No more. I want to rest again. Then at the office in mid-morning, the rest urge overtakes me once again and I stretch out in a reclining chair. This happens again after lunch and I feel really guilty about "over-resting." I guess it is "back to the medics" for me to get them to tell me what has happened and to restore my energy as best they can. I have great respect for and confidence in my doctor friends. They are great.

ADVANCING YEARS

Now that term is a euphemism. A euphemism is a use of words that make something seem better than the normal words commonly used would make it appear. Some call it maturing. Some call it aging. The Bible refers to a person going through it as being full of years. Another expression in wide use is senior citizen. But they all mean simply you are getting old.

But then I got to thinking. How does this affect you? How do you know you are full of years? Here are some of the sure signs of some of the things that happen — by their appearance you shall know them. Your body develops many unexplained spots — and lots of mysterious knots. I call it the age of spots and knots. Another thing is that your veins (especially on your hands) stand out and they get prominent and blue. I remember they did that on old man Corrigan up the street from me when I was a boy. Another thing, your ankles swell at the end of the day. The skin and flesh on your neck sags and even your wrinkles have wrinkles. You begin to stoop over and lose height — you get shorter. Then, too, the spring goes out of your step and you tend to either shuffle or plod. Sometimes it is a cross between the two and it becomes a "pluffle." It is also true that you cut more easily. Brush against something hard and it will either cause a red place or it might even bleed a bit. Then, too, your eyesight begins to get worse. Glasses, then bifocals. Then trifocals and one eye is farsighted while the other is just the opposite. And among men the hearing gets so much worse. Most women hear even better as they get old but not men. There are lots more but too delicate to discuss. But if you have noticed any of those listed then you may know that the Bible was right — you have become full of years.

LOOKING BACKWARD

One of the things said so often and critically of older folks is that they seem to dwell so much on things past. They talk about yesteryear. To me, there seems to be logic for this approach, even though it may not please a lot of folks listening to such accounts. One version of our life span is that it, on the average, covers three score and ten years. That, to my best reckoning, is 70 years. If that be an accurate assessment, then when a fellow has attained 36 years of age, he is just over the halfway mark and is headed out. Thus, he has more history than he has future. When he talks, he discusses what has happened rather than what may happen and this gives rise to the saying about old folks dwelling in the past. When you get there, you realize it is not too bad, for lots of things have happened and some of them you like to dwell on because they were pleasurable and others you like to mention because you are glad they are over.

ON ADVANCING YEARS

I sat near where two standing ladies were busily talking to each other. They were not over eight or ten feet from me. They heard each other perfectly. I heard not one sound from either and they were talking rather earnestly it seemed. Now, vision is another thing. Men's vision fails and so does that of some women but by no means all. The result is that when you are somewhere and someone speaks to you, you don't recognize the face because you can't see well enough. And of course when you do see the face, you cannot hook it up to a name. So always sit with your back to the door so you won't see the folks face-to-face as they enter.

LOOKING GOOD

Lester Maddox once said with a great bit of truth that there were three stages of life, youth, middle age, and "You're looking good."

84 GOING ON 85

Remember when you were a child and somebody would ask you how old you were and your answer would be like this, "I'm 7 years old, going on 8." Well, I am now 84 going on 85 which with my present state of health, I doubt seriously that I will ever make it. But we shall see. A miracle may occur. Who knows? My grandson is 8 years old now and looking back I was 8 years old in 1918, and going on 9.

PERSPECTIVE REVISITED

I guess perspective is the way you see things from where you are. Our perspectives on life are quite different as we see it from different ages. When one is young he views life with great wonder and anticipation, guessing what it holds for the observer down the years ahead which seem almost unlimited. The young person sees friends, conjectures about school, about marriage, about a life work and many, many other unknowns. Immortality is on the back burner if it is cooking at all.

Then with the gradual, and finally the not-too-gradual, passage of time the observer comes to appreciate the hackneyed verse which goes:

I'm growing old, my youth is spent,
My-get-up-and-go has got up and went,
But when I look back, I have to grin
At the places my get-up-and-go has been.

The view changes and all of a sudden you realize the perspective has become one giving an entirely different view. You know what your education, marriage, family, occupation and place of abode will be and instead of looking forward with fervent anticipation you begin to look backward with fond and sometimes really glowing memories. Some of us dwell on these memories too much and give ourselves over to boring and continuing references to things in the past. Others simply quietly reflect on what has happened, taking pride in some of it and being filled with regret because of things which might have been and weren't. I have been trying to figure out which is the best perspective, the exciting prospects of the unknown that lies ahead or the pleasure of memories of things that took place. I sort of forget my youthful

135

anticipatory musings because they are in the distant past and I seem, at least from where I now sit, to like the backward look. The mystery is gone and I can select only the good things to dwell on and cast aside those instances where all those mistakes were made.

By the way, immortality has definitely moved up to one of the front burners.

GIVING THANKS FOR A PIG VALVE

It has now been 13 years since Drs. Charlie Hatcher and Ellis Jones cut out the aortic valve from my heart and replaced it with a valve taken from a pig. I wrote both of them and thanked them for doing the fine job they did as I felt it would last but a year or two at most. I have always wanted to know the procedure but hesitated to ask. Did they put a Poland China hog on the table next to mine and take his out (or maybe it was hers out) and plunk it over to the next table and hook it up to me, or did they have a bank of them to use in such cases? If it was from a bank it seems the valve would have been dead for some time and wouldn't respond when inserted. Thank goodness that was their problem and not mine, though I guess basically it was my problem and not theirs. It worked. Thank the Lord.

DENTISTS

Dentistry and medicine, as well as the law, are good professions if properly practiced. I am going to start with dentists. Recently I had a pain in the last tooth on the bottom on the left-hand side, called a molar, I believe. My dentist is Dr. Nick Smith and he is great. I bet you thought I was going to say Dr. Vincio Velocipede, right out of Rome, Italy. But Nick is a local guy, the proud son of Roy Smith, who was my dentist prior to him. Nick has an office on Peachtree Road, just beyond Lenbrook Square, on the left-hand side. He acquired an old residence and converted it into a very fine and well-appointed office.

I had a pain in my lower jaw as I told you and I got Nick to x-ray it. He said it was abscessed and had to come out. The appointment was for last Thursday at 11:30 and I dreaded it every moment from that time until it was done. When I got there and before he started in on it, I said, "Level with me, Nick, is this going to be painful?" For I had already thought that it would be and that I would scream like a wounded eagle. His reply was, "No, you won't even know when I pull it out." I said sotto voce to myself, "Nick, you are a great dentist, but you will lie."

But he did not lie. He deadened the whole area, including my tongue and my lip, with some sort of stuff. He said, "Now, Henry, if it's all in one piece, I can remove it at one time, but if it crumbles, I'll have to dig it out." I said a prayer, "Lord, let it be a one-piece job." He was exactly right. There was no pain. It was in one piece but he decided to cut it in half and remove it one-half at a time. I could not believe it. I told him, "Nick, I take it all back. You're not a liar like I thought you were." He is an honest man and literally the best dentist I know right now.

The dentists I've had, along with his father, Roy, were the following: Deneen McCormack, Homer Davis, Hubbard Turner, Allan Davis. Allan was one of my favorite folks and was married to Anna Jeanne Blackburn, who is continuing to be my real good friend and who bakes the best apple cakes I ever tasted. I call her "AJBD" because those are her initials and she is a wonderfully fine person in every way. Allan died way yonder too young and I treasure the memory of our friendship. If you ever have to have a tooth pulled, don't do anything until you have talked to Nick Smith. He is probably the best dentist in Georgia.

DOCTORS

It has been my good fortune to have had fine doctors over the years. I've had more things wrong than the Mayo Clinic has ever seen. In my childhood I had several doctors to whom my parents took me. But then in my maturity, I have had Bob Whipple, Linton Bishop, Bruce Logue, who is now retired and who placed me in the hands of Dr. Paul Seavey, than whom there is no whomer. Paul has suffered an illness that is speeding up his retirement and he has placed me in the hands of Dr. Jonathan Major, who will probably succeed Paul as the big daddy rabbit in the Emory Clinic. I like him and thus far he and I have gotten along together real well. I hope he has the ability to keep me alive but only if he can make me feel better along with it. The way I feel today as I dictate this, death cannot come too soon. I won't describe it further than that but it is true.

Doctors come in different varieties. Some will hurry you in and out and others will offer sympathetic ears and you feel that they are really working in your interest. For years Dr. Bruce Logue was my doctor. As was Linton Bishop. Bruce and I are close personal friends and he was the number one coronary expert and probably now knows more about it than anybody would believe. Due to failing health, he retired and now lives up the street from me right near the Capital City Country Club. Although he no longer totes a black bag, he still has the sympathetic ear and the good judgment to stop by my house and inquire as to my health whenever he's down this way. He and his good wife Carolyne are just plain wonderful folks. I don't know what the future holds for me and doctors, but I hope Major and I make it out well together. He is personable and I'm sure he must be competent. If he can come up with an answer to my shingles, he'll move up to the number one doctor in the U.S.A.

GETTING READY

I have this week lost two of my friends by death. Each was a tad older than I but I have known them ever since grammar school days. I said to myself, Bowden, get ready old boy because the next scoop may have you in it with your right leg hanging out. I am not afraid to die though I am not making close friends with the Grim Reaper. It is sort of like this as I see it, the first event is birth, then comes your experiences in life. I have gotten through the first and a heck of a lot of the second. I know nobody who has enjoyed the first two of these three things any more than I. I have had a wonderful parentage, terrific experiences since than and I am ready to take on the third whenever the Good Lord says come. He put me here and it is He who will have to take me away. Suicide is not in my list of things to do. I have had some rough times like I am having now with this five-year illness, but I am not complaining because some bad has to come with the good.

TERMINAL ILLNESS

Had a call from a lady's son. I had known him and his mama for many years. He said she was in the hospital suffering from multiple, terminal cancers and wanted to see me. I went out right away. She seemed in good enough spirits and we talked for a good while together. I reminded her that it was 26 years before that her husband was similarly ill and I went out to sit with him. He wanted to tell me that he knew the end was nigh and that he held no grudges nor hard feelings against anyone. He was resigned to his fate and did die within the next day or two afterward. She, too, knew her situation and when I told her I hoped she would soon regain her full measure of health, she replied that she knew she would not.

This made me conjecture as to whether I would prefer to die suddenly or with some advanced warning, not necessarily a lengthy illness, but at least some knowledge that death was not far off. I decided that I would prefer the sudden passing approach provided it does not occur while driving so as to cause damage or injury to others. My own wife, Ellen, died one Saturday night in her sleep. It was mighty easy on the dying person but shocking in the extreme to the survivors and traumatic. Don't know how others feel but these are my sentiments.

MY HEALTH

People keep asking me, "Bowden, what's wrong with you? Why don't you get out of bed?" That prompted me to tell you what is wrong with me. Let's start at the top. Part of my pituitary gland was removed, as a result of which the hormones normally supplied by the blood stopped coming. I therefore take every morning at breakfast time eight artificial hormone pills to supply the missing ones. It's hard to get them down, but I do. Next, I am in the fifth year now from the atrocious pain of shingles in the left side of my forehead extending back into the back of my head. It is excruciatingly painful and the pain is not relieved by scratching or pills or anything else I have found thus far.

Next, my eyesight has just about gone and I am suffering with what they call macular degeneration. This means you can't see. I cannot read the paper nor my mail, and I cannot watch television because I can't see it. It's difficult to recognize my friends when they come into the room and all in all it's a pretty miserable thing.

Next, I have had pacemakers put in my heart twice. I had a valve in my heart which was replaced by a pig valve and seems to be working all right and, as I said before, I feel the pig must have been a Poland China because I feel much more kindly to both of those countries than I had before.

Next, I fell the other day while brushing my teeth and broke a rib on the lower right side which you do not bind up. But the pain you suffer for about six weeks I am told. That will be August 1 before I get any relief from it.

Next, as is true with most people who get old, your knee joints give out along with other joints and your balance is maintained with difficulty. My ankles are swollen and so are my hands and wrists. I take medicine every other day calculated to remove liquid from your physiognomy and let me tell you, it works. I am bedridden with wonderful nurses 24 hours a day. All of the above accompanied by rather consistent constipation does not make you get up in the morning alert with anticipation for what the day is going to hold. I have simply adopted an attitude which is expressed in the old expression, "The fleas come with the dog."

THE WAY IT IS

My mother died some while back at 91. Her memory by then was a bit spotty. I stopped by to see her one afternoon late just to see how she was doing. We visited together for a while and finally she said, "Son, tell me, are you married?" I said, "Why of course I am married, Mama. You know Ellen and our four children and recall our times together and how many times they have all spent the night with you." She simply said, "Well, that is the way it is, I guess. You never tell me anything anymore."

DEATH

Many persons are afraid to die. I do not share that feeling. It is not that I now welcome death, but when it comes I do not fear it. Any human life is made up of experiences. The first is birth. It happens to all human beings. The last is death and it too, happens to us all. While in youth and the adventuresome middle age of life, the death experience is abhorrent to contemplate, but as you get older your body shows the wear and tear of its use over the years and it emphasizes the temporary nature of existence on earth and really makes of death by no means the bug-a-boo that is constituted when you were young and vigorous.

Now mind you, I am not asking for death, because the Great God of the Universe has blessed me with more than my share of health and vigor. As long as I can maintain it, I wish to continue to live and to experience life here to the fullest and to serve others. I can imagine, however, that under the circumstances as they may develop in the time left to me, I may welcome death as a great relief. The basic main desire on the part of most of us is to keep birth and death, the two inexorable events in all lives, as far apart in time as humanly possible.

KNEE-DEEP IN THE JORDAN

When one is young, death seems about the most abhorrent

thing you could contemplate, but when you are stricken with years and the cold waters of Jordan are up to your kneecaps the prospect, as I have experienced it, does not appear nearly so bad. It is not that you want to die, but it is that you know that in the orderly processes of life when you reach a certain age, it is closer than it ever was and you might as well face it. The principal concerns that I have are about like this I guess: (a) I want to die quickly and not have a lingering death cycle; (b) I prefer to be with my loved ones at the time of my passing; (c) I do not want to die of a dread disease such as cancer, T.B., Alzheimer's or AIDS; (d) I wish to die in such a way as not to injure others or damage anyone's property, i.e., in an automobile wreck where my car may have hit and caused injury or death to another; and (e) I want to be "with it" right up to the end so that I am conscious of what is going on, recognize my family and friends and can figuratively lie down on my couch, pull the covers about me and quietly acknowledge His presence and purpose when the angel comes.

[Henry Bowden died peacefully in his own bed on February 17, 1997.]

Appendix

From: 'Here's the Dope'

HENRY BOWDEN'S COLUMN IN THE EMORY WHEEL, MAY 11, 1933

W e include the following to show that Henry Bowden's wit and exuberance long preceded Random Observations.

—*Publisher*

Bowden note — Philip Alston broke up the Lawyer-Preacher ballgame the other day with a homer in the seventh. I write it first as it should be written, then as a lawyer would write it, then as a med would depict it, and lastly as a preacher would set it down. Here goes:

THE CORRECT WAY

In the final frame with the Barristers trailing by a three run margin and the bases full, Phil Alston, rookie legal first sacker, clouted the pellet squarely on the trademark over the left centerfield fence for four sacks. He clouted the Lawyers to a victory over the Parsons and himself to a permanent niche in the legal hall of fame.

145

NOW AS A LAWYER WOULD WRITE IT

Now come the Lawyers, and in the final, last and seventh inning do come to bat and find that they are three (3) runs, scores, tallies, or markers in arrears of the number of runs already acquired by the opposition, other side, Preachers. And, whereas, it has become necessary that four (4) of said runs, scores, tallies, or markers be acquired to accord the said Lawyers a victory and abatement of said opposition, one Philip Henry Alston, county of Fulton, State of Georgia, with due malice aforethought did take into his hands a bat. And, further, the said Philip Henry Alston of said county and state, did hit, smack, clout, knock, frap, rap, and romp on aforementioned baseball against the peace and dignity of the said opposition, the other side, Preachers. And yet, further, the said ball did without any outside interference, aid, or assistance sail, fly, and float over the fourth section of the left centerfield fence. And as a result of such flying, sailing, and floating, the said ball was lost forever. And in view of the fact that all three (3) bases had men upon them rightfully, lawfully, duly, and legally, their runs counted and the said Lawyers were declared victors in the amount of eight and seven (8-7).

WHAT A MED WOULD SAY

In the final extremity of the second baseball game between the Lawyers Hilkitis and the Preachers Parkerias, the Parkerias were in the lead by a perceptible margin of three runs. With the bases in a hypothetical state of intoxication, Philip Alston, who plays on the right lateral side of the diamond shaped playing field, came to bat brandishing an elongated, rounded proboscis shaped piece of ash wood. It was apparent that he was free from myopia. He focused the retinal regions of his optic member on the oncoming spheroid. He swung and his ash wood made a violent connection with the dorsal surface of the spheroid. The ball traveled superficially and in a left diagonal direction toward the third segment left of the mid regional fence. It lifted over this apparent obstruction and gave the hitter and those ahead of him free circulation of the primary, secondary, tertiary, and domiciliar bases. This gave the Hilkitis aggregation a slight, but perceptible, victory over the Parkerias.

THE PREACHERS' VERSION

And when the seventh inning had come, and the game was nigh unto an end, the Lawyers arose to see what could be done, and woe was round about them, and they were sorely disheartened and afraid. The ministers and those who had come up with them and were on the sidelines cheering, had tilted the balances and had found the Lawyers wanting, yea, even three runs. But lo, there came a man named Philip, son of Philip of the house of Alston, and when the bases were full with people and when the ball was thrown to him, he bided his time and he smote it on the back thereof, with a sound and lustful vigor. And when they had arisen and had seen what was around about them, the ball was moreover resting in the valley of the outermost regions of the diamond. And the lawyers, and all those who had come up with them were exceedingly joyful and straightway they went out into the wilderness of the library where they did gloat and boast in victory moreover.

On Turning 21

A LETTER FROM HENRY BOWDEN TO HIS GRANDDAUGHTER, JANE FIDLER, SEPTEMBER 16, 1991.

Dear Jane,

I did enjoy so much the chance to drive you back to Hollins on September 8. It was fun being with you and the fact that you drove all the way was a help too. You were right, we could not have gotten all your stuff in my car and I am glad I had the truck available. Irene is a faithful vehicle and held it all very well even though we could not see through the rear view mirror with all your stuff piled up.

Your next birthday, littlest one, is the one on which you become 21 years old. That is a meaningful birthday for us all. I attained it in 1931 and I can recall it vividly now. I got to thinking of some things I would certainly do if I were 21 again and those are the ideas I want to now pass along to you. Some of them are my own real conclusions, others I have heard, talked about or read about, but wherever it is they come from to me, they are good and I heartily recommend them to my fine grandgirl.

(a) First, I would give 20 minutes each day to some special physical exercise. Happiness depends on health, health depends on digestion, digestion depends on blood, good blood depends on circulation, and circulation depends on exercise. Some fellow I read about said he would rather have as a father a robust burglar than a narrow chested, consumptive bishop. Cultivate exercises which are natural. Laugh a lot, yawn a lot, sing a lot, stretch and walk a lot. Laugh after each meal.

(b) Next, I would strive to be an original thinker. It seems at 10 we wonder, 20 we imagine, 30 cogitate, 40 think, 50 have an idea or two, 60 two ideas, 70 work on one idea. If you go wrong, you first think wrong. Don't take things for granted...think them through. Think your way through prejudice, precedent, custom, habit, style, fashion, and anything else. If you think your way into something, it usually is not hard to think your way out again. Have faith in your conclusions based on thought. Be original.

(c) Next, I would steer my life by a few just plain fundamental convictions. These are expressed in such words as God, Love, Truth, Right, Law, Immortality. Don't be afraid of platitudes. Right is right and wrong is wrong. Apply it. Martin Luther came through because he had strong convictions. Never carry tolerance to the point where it means full license. There are lots of things you should just plain not tolerate.

(d) Next, sweetheart, I would have a clear conviction as to the sovereign value of my soul in the presence of God. When God became human He was in the person of Christ. The Bible says every man has the ability to be like Christ, but man also has the ability to become like Judas. Each of us is here as divinely as any other who is here. The old woman seen in the bank the other day is as much a soul as you or I. It takes a whole solar system to make a strawberry — a whole God to make a man. Man is God's chosen creature. Make God proud of you.

(e) Be sure and strive to put quality into every word and deed, for a true Christian is one who does ordinary things in an extraordinary way. Twenty centuries ago a carpenter built a cross. Little did he know it would become a symbol for all that it has. Make quality the symbol for which you are recognized.

(f) Then, Jane, try to achieve one splendid success in some realm of human effort. Select something you wish to do and know more about it than anyone else. Make a better mousetrap. Booker T. Washington told the blacks after being freed to let down their buckets where they were.

(g) Try to crowd at least one kind act into every 24-hour period. You see, grandgirl, kindness is the velvet of social intercourse, oil in life's machinery, the controlling spring on the slamming door. It is sort of like the burlap in everyday's packing case, the carpet on life's floor that softens the sound. It is the satin lining in the silver casket, the plush on the chair, the green grass growing in the pebbles along the road, the touch of an angel's hand.

(h) Please, Jane, try to live in the light of every grand experience. Moments are sweet and divine too; there are sunbursts. Rain is wet but also beautiful. Stars sometimes are like living diamonds, events often crowd eternity into an hour. Live to know beauty all around you.

(i) And don't ever forget to make two or three good friends among old people. They know the way, have often learned the meaning of life, have been along the road you are traveling, and would love to count you among their few favorites. They will assist in your plans, they yearn for the comfort of your confidence, and I assure you they will glory in your success. They will boast to their friends about you. I know this because I am one of those old people I am talking about.

(j) Don't fail to read over at least once each year the four gospels. They are the heart of the Bible. All in the Old

Testament leads up to the gospels and all of the New Testament grows out of the four gospels and the Acts.

(k) I won't be much longer, dear one, but I would identify myself with some great, just, even though unpopular, cause. Courage is some fine test of character. Dare to be different, to deny, to dispute. Not just to be obstinate, but to take a stand you know deep down is just and right. You may be lonely in so doing, but I would rather you stand still than to creep and crawl with the mob. They may swear at you to begin with, but they will swear by you in the end.

(l) Spend a little time each day with the really beautiful. Keep a flower on your desk. Keep a notebook with gems in it. Read it daily and change it as you feel you should. Add to it also. Read a pretty poem every day for a month and at the end you probably will have memorized it. Please give the flower of your youth to Christ. Begin with Him. Don't wait and turn over the ashes to Him. There is no way you can understand all of Him, but surrender to Him anyway and try to keep a small picture of Him in your room where you may see it daily. Look at His face and His hands that did so much good for the world.

You are a sophomore this year and I know you are gratified at this. But I caution you not to be sophomoric. A person who is sophomoric thinks she knows it all. Be assured that you do not, for no one knows it all.

I understand you have a boyfriend, a beau, a sweetheart, or whatever it is they call them these days. If so, I am delighted. But let me add that if this is so, have a respect for him as you wish him to have a similar respect for you. By no means give yourself over to him prior to marriage. You will regret it if you do. It is not the proper way despite newspaper articles saying it differently. You listen to me this time.

I hope you read with profit and approval the things I am saying to you, littlest one, for they come from my heart to one whom I love dearly and one who I hope has some of that same feeling for your old Grandpa Bowden.

151